Study Guide

WILLIAM E. DOYLE
El Camino College
Torrence, CA

LISTENING TO MUSIC

Jay D. Zorn
University of Southern California

PRENTICE HALL, ENGLEWOOD CLIFFS, NEW JERSEY 07632

Editorial/production supervision: **Elaine Price**
Supplements acquisition editor: **Ann Knitel**
Manufacturing buyers: **Herb Klein/Dave Dickey**
Cover design: **Donna Wickes**

A Division of Simon & Schuster
Englewood Cliffs, New Jersey 07632

Printed in the United States of America

10 9 8 7 6 5 4 3 2 1

ISBN 0-13-538380-3

Prentice-Hall International (UK) Limited, *London*
Prentice-Hall of Australia Pty. Limited, *Sydney*
Prentice-Hall Canada Inc., *Toronto*
Prentice-Hall Hispanoamericana, S.A., *Mexico*
Prentice-Hall of India Private Limited, *New Delhi*
Prentice-Hall of Japan, Inc., *Tokyo*
Simon & Schuster Asia Pte. Ltd., *Singapore*
Editora Prentice-Hall do Brasil, Ltda., *Rio de Janeiro*

TABLE OF CONTENTS

PREFACE

This manual is intended to accompany Jay Zorn's *Listening to Music* . It is designed to help the student master the information contained within the textbook and to provide a set of questions that are representative of the course material.

The Study Guide is intended to help you, the student, understand the world of concert music. I have always felt that a music appreciation course is one of the most important classes which can be offered by a music department.

What should a non-music major learn in a music appreciation course? First, the student must become acquainted with the musical vocabulary. Second, the student should be taught how to listen to music at the "aware" level. Unfortunately, all too often the student is overwhelmed with information and ends up feeling indifferent towards Western concert music. This affects the third aspect, which is attitude. That is why this Study Guide was written - to help focus the attention of the student upon the key aspects of the material.

The Study Guide is organized into three main sections:

SUMMARY - key terms and concepts, overview of the chapter, highlights. The main points of the chapter are reviewed in the order presented in the text. This is an ideal place to refer back to when you are preparing for an exam in addition to the summary at the end of the textbook chapter.

STUDY QUESTIONS - matching, fill in the blank, and multiple choice. The purpose of this section is to check your understanding of the material in the chapter before you take an examination in class.

LISTENING SELF-TEST - questions based on the musical selections discussed in the text. Use this section while you are listening to the music. If you are unable to answer any of the questions, re-read the chapter and re-take the test.

Special thanks to Jay Zorn for his suggestions, to Ann Knitel and her staff for their help in preparing this manuscript, and to Sue-Ann Calhoun, Bruce Tellier, and Allan Tudzin for their suggestions.

Dr. William E. Doyle

Prelude/Chapter 1. The Musical Process

Summary

Musical process begins with the composer's ideas. Then the musical materials are shaped, put into a coherent form. Finally they are notated. Performers read and interpret these symbols and re-create the composer's ideas though the performance medium for you - the listener.

How do you listen to music? Music, like all the arts, can accommodate all viewpoints. What you hear depends on the way you listen and on your focus.

There are five levels of listening.

1. Sensory - effortless listening.
2. Emotional - private world, emotional response.
3. Contextual - music is associated with an event.
4. Script - making up a story to fit the music.
5. Aware - understand the music, can enjoy it for its own sake.

Study Questions

1. The process of writing musical ideas on paper is called:

    a. rhythm
    b. expression
    c. notation
    d. texture

2. Which of the following is not a musical material?

    a. melody
    b. harmony
    c. texture
    d. composition

3. The performance medium is:

    a. the same as a musical form
    b. the basic musical idea
    c. the voices or instruments used
    d. a musical symbol

4. The most important link in the musical process is:

   a. the listener
   b. the composer
   c. the performer
   d. the critics

5. What level of listening "allows your brain to idle in neutral"?

   a. sensory
   b. contextual
   c. script
   d. aware

6. Which level allows you to follow musical lines and patterns?

   a. sensory
   b. contextual
   c. emotional
   d. aware

Chapter 2. Becoming an Aware Concertgoer

Summary

There is no difference between a symphony orchestra and a philharmonic orchestra. The difference is in the name only. A symphony or philharmonic orchestra is a large musical ensemble comprised of strings, brass, woodwinds, and percussion.

A chamber orchestra is a small group of musicians - usually 20 to 40 in number. Today, 2 to 6 musicians generally perform chamber music concerts. The term chamber music has been in use since the late 1600's when small groups of musicians played in the chambers and courts of palaces.

A recital usually features one or two musicians. Vocal ensembles can range from large and small choirs to madrigal groups and church choirs. A madrigal is a piece of Elizabethan vocal music for a small ensemble.

Opera is musical theater built around a libretto or a story.
Ballet creates its effects by combining various art forms with specific dance steps and movements.

Information regarding concerts can be obtained from newspapers, mailing lists, season subscriptions, and the box office.

To prepare for a concert it is best to acquaint yourself with the music prior to the concert.

The conductor's duties include more than just setting the tempo and beating time. The conductor must coordinate, interpret, and balance the ensemble. A baton is generally used for maximum visibility. The first beat of any pattern is called the downbeat. The beats are organized into patterns or meters, generally, in groups of two, three or four. The left hand of the conductor is used to indicate expression to the orchestra. Cueing is the process whereby musicians are signalled to begin playing. The term "opus" refers to the cataloguing of a composer's works.

Study Questions

1. Chamber music can be found:

    a. in small concert halls
    b. in the courts of palaces
    c. in today's concert halls
    (d) all of the above

2. Solo recitals are most commonly given by:

   a. one or two musicians
   b. singers and pianists
   c. violinists
   d. all of the above

3. Large choirs:

   a. vary in size from forty to four hundred
   b. perform only in churches
   c. are used at outdoor concerts
   d. perform only with instrumental accompaniment

4. "A cappella" means: – without accompaniment

   a. a small choir
   b. in the style of the church
   c. the use of instruments
   d. all of the above

5. Church choirs perform:

   a. ~~only~~ the greatest masterpieces
   b. ~~only~~ in church
   c. ~~only~~ in concert halls
   d. ~~musical theater~~ all of the above

6. Opera is a combination of:

   a. vocal forms
   b. instrumental forms
   c. art forms
   d. choirs

7. The left hand of a conductor is used to:

   a. indicate expression
   b. indicate cueing
   c. both a. and b.
   d. none of the above

Soprano
Alto
Tenor
Bass

Church Choir - sing sacred music: Not Secular

Chapter 3. The Interaction of Musical Elements

Summary

Characteristics of Music (Sound) = S

1.)

Terms:

The elements of music are:

Rhythm - duration of sound. They are either prominent or weak beats.
Tempo - the rate of speed.
Metronome - a device that measures the speed or tempo.
Moderato - a tempo that is close to our own pulse.
Tempos - can be either steady and/or flexible.
Rubato - the speeding up and/or slowing down of the tempo.
Meter - the rhythmic groupings of duple, triple, and less common meters.
Syncopation - unexpected accents that occur off of the main beat.
Ostinato - a repetitive rhythmic pattern.
Silence - also an important part of music.

Pitch - melody and harmony both are pitch related.
Melody - a succession of individual pitches.
Melodies - prominent and not prominent are two designations of melodies.
Musical building blocks are comprised of melodic motives and rhythmic motives.
Cadence - an arrival at a resting place in the music.
Ornamentation- a matter of prevailing taste or fashion whereby the melody is decorated.
Trills - are rapid alternation between two pitches. It is considered a decoration or ornamentation.

Repetition, imitation, sequence are three devices used by composers.
Imitation - a form of repetition. For example, canons and rounds are highly imitative.
Sequences - another form of repetition. For example, taking a melodic motive and repeating it higher or lower.
Scales - a group of ascending or descending pitches.
Major and minor dominate the music of the Western world up until the late eighteenth century.

Harmony - is a result of the combinations of pitches sounded simultaneously.
Chord - is a series of three pitches simultaneously.
Consonant - a stable chord or harmonic structure.
Dissonant - a clashing chord or harmonic structure.

Musical Textures - the layers of sound that combine to weave a musical fabric.
Monophonic - one melody all by itself.
Homophonic - a melody with a chordal accompaniment.
Polyphonic - several independent lines, or melodies, that sound (weave) together.

Musical notation consists of pitch notation, staff, clefs, grand staff, the notation of duration and of scales.

Study Questions

D 1. The highness or lowness of a tone is called:

a. timbre
b. melody
c. rhythm
(d.) pitch

B 2. Ascending or descending notes are called:

a. tone color
(b.) scales
c. tempo
d. meter

D 3. To get louder or softer is to alter the:

a. pitch
b. rhythm
c. structure
(d.) volume

A 4. The groupings of beats into patterns is called:

(a.) meter
b. tempo
c. tone
d. form

D 5. One type of harmony is consonant, the other is:

a. monophonic
b. polyphonic
c. octatonic
(d.) dissonant

Opening Music: Mozart: Requiem Introit

C 6. The rate of speed that the music moves at is called:

a. meter
b. rhythm
(c.) tempo
d. duration

A 7. Musical building blocks are comprised of melodic motives and:

(a.) rhythmic motives
b. cadences
c. harmonic motives
d. tone color

C 8. An arrival at a resting place in the music is called a(n):

a. pause
b. stop
(c.) cadence
d. tempo

A 9. Ornamentation is a matter of prevailing taste or fashion whereby the:

(a.) melody is decorated
b. melody is left alone
c. notes are reversed
d. melody is alternated

C 10. Trills are rapid alternation between:

a. two instruments
b. two pianos
(c.) two pitches
d. none of the above

B 11. A group of ascending or descending pitches is:

a. the basis for all nonWestern music
(b.) called a scale
c. harmonic structure
d. formal constraint

C 12. What system has dominated the music of the Western world?

a. Gregorian chant
b. the theories of Handel
(c.) major and minor tonality
d. church modes

B

13. What results from the combinations of pitches sounded simultaneously?

    a. melody
    (b.) harmony
    c. sequence
    d. rhythm

C

14. Three or more notes sounded simultaneously creates:

    a. tension
    b. consonance
    (c.) a chord
    d. dissonance

Chapter 4. Performing Media: Instruments, Voices, and Ensembles

Summary

Performers bring music to life. All voices and musical instruments need 3 basic components to function: an energy source, a vibrating element, and a resonating chamber. For example, with the human voice the air is the energy source. The vocal cords provide the vibrating element while the oral cavity is the resonating chamber.

Categories of instruments are the strings, woodwinds, brass, percussion, keyboards, and electronic families of instruments.

What distinguishes one instrument from another is its timbre or tone color. Each instrument has a different timbre or difference in the quality of their tone.

Various performing media include solo recitals, ensembles (brass, woodwind, etc.), a symphony orchestra, and a wind ensemble.

The string section consists of violins, violas, celli, and string bass. The use of pizzicato refers to a plucked bow technique used by the strings.

The woodwind section consists of piccolo, flutes, oboes, English horn, clarinets, bassoons, contrabassoon, and saxophones.

The brass section is made up of trumpets, horn, trombone, tuba. Mutes are used to change the timbre of the brass instruments.

The percussion section is composed of instruments that are pitched and non-pitched. A timpani, for example, is pitched because it can be tuned to specific pitches or notes.

The development of the orchestra:
Before the seventeenth century no standard orchestra existed.
The Roman Catholic Church was mainly interested in vocal music.
Chamber ensembles were the main instrumental groups before the development of the symphony orchestra.

Around 1600, Gabrieli began to specify which instruments were to be used in his music. This is the beginning of instrumentation and orchestration. Monteverdi built on Gabrieli's ideas.

A concerto consists of a small chamber ensemble and a soloist.
A concerto grosso is a small chamber ensemble with several soloists.

Late eighteenth century, every major European court had its own small orchestra for entertainment purposes.

Haydn and Mozart contributed to the birth of the modern orchestra. Inspired by Beethoven, other nineteenth century composers continued to enlarge the orchestra.

With the invention of valves on brass instruments, many composers began to write prominent parts for various brass instruments. Other composers, such as Berlioz, began to focus on the variety of instrumental timbres in the orchestra. In order to meet the performance demands of the late nineteenth century, orchestras hired virtuoso performers to play in every section.

In 1913, Stravinsky gave new prominence to the percussion section with his ballet The Rite of Spring.

The wind ensemble consists primarily of wind instruments and an occasional string. American bands, like those of Sousa, spread the popularity of band music in the early twentieth century.

Keyboard instruments include the organ, harpsichord, and the piano.

In the category of electronic instruments you will find synthesizers and the like.

The human voice is an "instrument" that has various designations. For female, from high to low, are sopranos, mezzo sopranos, and altos. The males are, from high to low, tenors, baritones, and bass.

Study Questions

1. Which of the following is not a component of musical sound:

   a. energy source
   b. resonating chamber
   (c.) tone color
   d. vibrating element

2. The quality of sound an instrument produces is called:

   a. melody
   (b) tone color
   c. pitch
   d. col legno

3. A string quartet has:

   a. two violins, one viola and one cello
   b. one violin, one viola, one cello, one bass
   c. two violins, two celli
   d. none of these

4. The symphony orchestra and wind ensemble are:

   a. about the same
   b. different only in size
   c. common large instrumental ensembles
   d. from the same time period

5. Which section is not part of the typical symphony orchestra:

   a. brass
   b. keyboards
   c. strings
   d. percussion

6. The second highest string instrument is called a:

   a. bass
   b. viola
   c. cello
   d. violin

7. To play pizzicato means to:

   a. play a trumpet
   b. pluck a string
   c. play a small flute
   d. none of these

8. Which instrument is not usually found in the woodwind section: Of the orchestra

   a. bassoon
   b. oboe
   c. saxophone
   d. clarinet

9. The brass instrument that plays the highest tones is:

   a. horn
   b. trombone
   c. trumpet
   d. flute

10. Which percussion instrument does not have a definite pitch:

a. timpani
b. xylophone
c. marimba
d. snare drum

11. According to the text, sound effects are:

a. created by the percussion section
b. an infinite variety of sounds
c. bird calls and street sounds
d. all of these

12. The orchestra of Haydn was:

a. only 30 pieces
b. part-time musicians
c. poorly trained and paid
d. all of these

13. The Roman Catholic Church was:

a. a leading employer of instrumentalists
b. only interested in vocal music
c. important in influencing the modern orchestra
d. all of these

14. Which composer was important in standardizing instrumentations?

a. Gabrieli
b. Vivaldi
c. Purcell
d. Monteverdi

15. Guarneri and Stradivari were:

a. court composers
b. violinists
c. string instrument makers
d. organists

16. A virtuoso is:

a. a composer
b. an instrument maker
c. a soloist with exceptional ability
d. a chamber ensemble

17. Vivaldi's concerto from the text book was written for:

   a. a violin
   b. two trumpets
   c. two oboes
   d. flute

18. The difference between a concerto and concerto grosso is:

   a. just the name
   b. the size of the orchestra
   c. the number of soloists
   d. when it was written

19. Which composer was most responsible for enlarging the orchestra?

   a. Beethoven
   b. Haydn
   c. Mozart
   d. Vivaldi

Fill in the Blank

20. ________ (composer) gave new prominence to the percussion section.

21. The ________ is the "king of instruments."

22. The ________ has thc lightest tone of all the keyboard instruments.

23. The highest male voice is called the ________ .

Listening Self-Test

Benjamin Britten, <u>Young Person's Guide to the Orchestra</u>.
Student's Cassette Tape. Side 1, no. 2.

24. The theme was originally written by:

   a. Vivaldi
   b. Handel
   c. Purcell
   d. Britten

25. Part two of the piece is a:

a. set of variations
b. fugue
c. feature for the entire orchestra
d. none of these

26. Part three of the piece is a:

a. set of variations
b. feature for the orchestra
c. fugue - musical fight
d. none of these

Gabrieli, "In ecclesiis" C.D No. 1., track 4.

27. This piece was written for:

a. organ
b. choir
c. soloists
d. all of these

28. Gabrieli keeps changing the:

a. instrumentation
b. orchestration
c. timbres
d. all of these

29. The type of composition is a(n):

a. organum
b. recitative
c. motet
d. chant

Chapter 5. An Introduction to Musical Styles

Summary

Musical styles reflect tastes and cultural attitudes. While composers of the same style period tend to reflect that style, there are exceptions. Some composers exhibit their creativity through innovation.

The important eras of musical style in Western art music are generally divided up as follows:

Middle Ages - from 450 - 1450
Renaissance - from 1450 - 1600
Baroque - from 1600 - 1750
Classical - from 1750 - 1820
Romantic - from 1820 - 1900
Twentieth Century - from 1900 to the present.

Study Questions

1. If the music of Mozart and Haydn sounds similar, we can say that the two composers had a similar:

    a. outlook on life
    b. attitude towards the arts
    c. style of musical composition
    d. music teacher

2. The dates of each style period are:

    a. approximations
    b. agreed upon for discussion purposes
    c. reflections of changes in thinking associated with the changes in society
    d. all of the above

3. The shortest time period was the:

    a. Middle Ages
    b. Renaissance
    c. Baroque Era
    d. Classical Era

4. Musical styles reflect the tastes and the:

   a. cultural attitudes
   b. economic status of composers
   c. religious inclinations of performers
   d. none of the above

5. Describing musical style periods requires:

   a. specification
   b. generalization
   c. studying representative artists
   d. both b. and c.

6. Which of the following is not a style period?

   a. Baroque
   b. Classical
   c. Neoclassical
   d. Renaissance

7. Stylistic similarities extend:

   a. only to music
   b. to the visual arts only
   c. to all the arts
   d. only to each style period

Chapter 6. Music Before 1600

Summary

The Middle Ages began with the decline of the Roman Empire and the invasions of the Germanic nations. While often called the Dark Ages, this period can also be called the "Age of Faith."

During this time, the Church became the center of learning. The Crusades were successful in changing the socioeconomic structures and cultural perspectives of Europe. An important development was the construction of the great Gothic cathedrals in the twelfth century (Notre Dame, Chartres, Salisbury, and Glouster).

Medieval Sacred Music

Gregorian chant, also called plainsong or plainchant, named after Pope Gregory I (590 - 604 A.D.).

1. Monophonic texture, unmeasured rhythm, Latin language used for text, and Hebrew, Roman, and Christian melodies were used.
2. Chant was used as part of the Mass
3. Music in the Church developed from Judaic roots (Hebrew service).

The Mass has two different kinds of texts - the Ordinary and the Proper.

1. The Ordinary (fixed text)
    a. Kyrie (prayer for mercy)
    b. Gloria (in praise of God's glory)
    c. Credo (statement of belief)
    d. Sanctus (proclaims God's holiness)
    e. Agnus Dei (lamb of God as source of mercy)
2. The Proper (changing text)
    a. Introit
    b. Gradual
    c. Alleluia (or Tract) Sequence
    d. Offertory
    e. Communion

Medieval Secular (nonreligious) Music

Monophonic songs were written by musical amateurs for entertainment purposes. These composers from different locations were known as:

1. Minstrels (Tenth century, France)
2. Troubadours (Twelfth century, So. France)
3. Trouveres (Twelfth century, No. France)
4. German Minnesingers (Fourteenth century, Germany)

Literary descriptions and paintings suggest that the songs were accompanied by a harp or lute (guitar-like).

Instruments of this period would include the flute, recorder, oboe-like instruments, various sizes of primitive violins, trumpets and drums.

In the Ninth century, another musical line was added to the monophonic chant, creating this new texture called polyphony, which means "many independent sounds."

The earliest polyphony at this time was known as organum.

1. At first the second voice was improvised.
2. Later, after 1000 A.D., it was indicated in the music.

Leonin and Perotin establish the "School of Notre Dame" and begin to sign their works. Previously, composers had been anonymous.

The Renaissance, 1450 - 1600

During this period there was a:

A. Renewed interest in ancient Greek and Roman arts and philosophy.
B. Inspired exploration, practical inventions, and discovery.
C. Individual achievement was cultivated under the spirit of "humanism."
D. Leonardo da Vinci (1452-1519) epitomizes the Renaissance man for his many and varied contributions to society (also Prince Macchiavelli).

Renaissance Music

Religious music was still predominant, but secular music was on the rise.

1. Small instrumental groups perform chamber music.
2. Court composers supply both the sacred and secular (chamber) music.

The Madrigal originated in Italy, became popular in England by the end of the Sixteenth century.

Its characteristics: text is in the language of the people (the vernacular); polyphony continues to dominate the texture; the music is written as many as 5 or 6 parts; use of counterpoint (melody against melody).

Palestrina was an important Renaissance composer. As a representative of the Renaissance style, his musical characteristics are:

a. seamless counterpoint
b. almost constant imitation
c. use of chant melodies
d. staggered entrances of voices

Study Questions

Fill in the Blank

1. Two other terms that refer to Gregorian chant are plainchant and plainsong.

2. Gregorian chant is monophonic in texture.

3. The texts for the Mass come from different groups. Texts that change throughout the year are called the proper, and those that remain the same are called the ordinary

4. Two of the principal groups of secular musicians in the Middle Ages were the troubadour in Southern France and the travere in Northern France.

5. The earliest type of polyphony that was created by adding a new melody to the monophonic chant is called organum

Matching

6. The text of the Gregorian chant was in this language.
   Latin
7. Pope who ordered his scholars to codify and notate chant. Gregory 1ST
8. The term that means "not dealing with religion."
   secular
9. Another name for the Middle Ages.
   Age of Faith
10. Music in the Church developed from these roots.
   Judaic

Gregory 1st
Latin
secular
vernacular
Italian
Age of Faith
John 1st
sacred
Judaic
Age of Reason
secular

Listening Self-Test

Gregorian Chant, "Kyrie" Tape #1, side 1, ex. 3. C.D. No. 1, track 1.

11. The texture of this chant is:

   (a) monophonic
   b. polyphonic
   c. organum
   d. homophonic

12. The language used is:

   a. the vernacular
   b. French
   (c) Latin
   d. German

13. The rhythm is:

   a. in a duple meter
   b. in a triple meter
   c. unmeasured and free
   d. march-like

14. The melody is sung:

   a. in unison
   b. by men only
   c. both a. and b.
   d. none of the above

Leonin, "Alleluia Pasha Nostrum" Tape #1, side 1, ex. 4. C.D. No. 1, track 2.

15. This work was composed by:

   a. Leonin
   b. Perotin
   c. Palestrina
   d. Pope Gregory

16. The texture of this work is:

   a. monophonic
   b. homophonic
   c. organum
   d. polyphonic

17. The lower voice holds the long tone while the upper voice:

   a. moves slower
   b. moves faster and more freely
   c. does the same as the lower voice
   d. none of the above

18. What portion of the Mass is this chant from:

   a. Proper
   b. Ordinary
   c. Matins
   d. Vespers

19. This composer was from the "School" of:

a. Chartres
b. Notre Dame
c. Salisbury
d. Rome

20. This is an example of:

a. secular music
b. entertainment music
c. sacred music
d. Medieval music

Fill in the Blank

21. The texture of Renaissance music is mainly polyphonic.

22. The principal intellectual movement in this period was Humanism

23. The Renaissance saw a renewed interest in ancient Greek and Roman art and philosophy.

24. Composers wrote for small instrumental groups called chamber music.

25. Court composers supplied both the sacred and secular music.

Matching

26. The madrigal originated in which country?
Italy

27. An instrument, somewhat similar to the guitar, that was popular in secular music.
lute

28. In a madrigal, how many voices can sing simultaneously?
5

29. Palestrina's career centered in which city?
Rome

30. Example of a "Renaissance man."
Leonardo da Vinci

lute
four
five
France
Naples
Rome
cornetto
Italy
da Vinci
Germany

Listening Self-Test

"Kyrie." Tape #1, side 2, Ex. 5. - C.D. No. 1, track 3.

31. The texture of this work is:

    a. monophonic
    b. homophonic
    c. polyphonic
    d. diatonic

32. The composer of this piece is:

    a. Leonin
    b. Perotin
    c. Palestrina
    d. anonymous

33. The amount of voices used are:

    a. one or two
    b. three or four
    c. five
    d. more than five

34. This piece is based on:

    a. an old Gregorian chant
    b. secular dance music
    c. music of the troubadours
    d. none of the above

35. This piece was composed:

    a. during the late 16th century
    b. during the late 15th century
    c. during the early 16th century
    d. during the late Middle Ages

36. It comes from the:

    a. Ordinary of the Mass
    b. Proper of the Mass
    c. the court of Prince Macchiavelli
    d. Vespers

37. The term for "melody against melody" that the composer uses is:

a. counterpoint
b. harmony
c. monophony
d. diatonic

Claudio MonteVerde - madrigal Italian
Thomas Morley " " English
Fa La La La

Chapter 7. From the Renaissance into the Baroque

Summary

The Protestant Reformation, starting in 1517, challenged the authority of the Church of Rome. Martin Luther, leader of this reformation, made two changes to make the liturgy more accessible. He translated the liturgy from Latin into German and added congregational singing to the service.

The Counter Reformation, by the Church of Rome in 1545, left a renewed interest in expressing the grandeur of the church through architecture. In short, a new image was created by the elaborate changes made to the churches and through the designs of the new, more elaborate Baroque-style churches.

Having experienced a period of self-renewal, the Catholic Church was to play a new role in the arts from 1600 to 1750.

As for the music of this period, it often sounds heavy, grand and expansive.

Study Questions

1. Which religious figure changed the function of music in the worship service?

    a. Pope Gregory 1st
    b. J. S. Bach
    c. Martin Luther
    d. King Henry VIII

2. Martin Luther's innovations included:

    a. translation of the liturgy into German
    b. translation of the liturgy into Italian
    c. adding congregational singing to the service
    d. both a. and c.

3. After the Reformation came the:

    a. Baroque Period
    b. Counter-Reformation
    c. Renaissance Period
    d. both a. and b.

4. The music of this period will tend to:

   a. resemble architecture in that it will be grand and ornate
   b. sound more complex
   c. return to the simplicity of the Middle Ages
   d. both a. and b.

5. The reforms of Martin Luther took place during the:

   a. Baroque
   b. Renaissance
   c. Middle Ages
   d. Council of Trent

6. The hymns of Luther were:

   a. borrowed from the Catholic Church
   b. easily sung
   c. in German
   d. both b. and c.

7. Architects during this time began to build:

   a. concert halls
   b. new churches
   c. public housing
   d. art galleries

8. In general, the music of the Baroque sounds:

   a. more grand and expressive
   b. longer
   c. more homophonic
   d. simpler

9. The concerto and concerto grosso are two important Baroque:

   a. buildings
   b. keyboards
   c. musical forms
   d. string instruments

10. Sequence, imitation, and elaborate ornamentation are all Baroque:

   a. rhythm devices
   b. expressive markings
   c. harmonic devices
   d. melodic devices

Chapter 8. Baroque Music

Summary

In the 1600's, Venice was the commercial maritime center of the world and it also was the host to many musical innovations in church services. Gabrieli's innovations included specification of instruments and expression markings.

The word Baroque is derived from the Portuguese word describing irregular pearls. The art of this period is often elaborate, decorative, and highly ornate. Music combining vocal and instrumental ensembles remained popular throughout the Baroque period.

The first full-length opera was staged around 1600 in northern Italy. The first public opera house was built in Venice in 1637. Monteverdi is credited with one of the earliest operas - Orfeo written in 1607.

The term libretto means "little book." It is the story or play upon which an opera is based. The Italian language, considered the most suitable language for singing, was the primary language of opera.

St. Paul, in 1565, declared that only men were to sing in church. This led to the practice of castration whereby young boys were then given the high female parts to sing.

Terms:

Antiphonal - music coming from several different directions.
Concertato Principle - contrasting groups of sound. This leads to the concert and to the concerto.
Recitativo - effective compromise between speech and singing.
Aria - solo song. Later, this would dominate the operas.
Usually in a three-part form known as A B A; a melodic A section, contrasting B section, return to the original A section.

Ensembles - could include duets, trios, and quartets.
Chorus - the full ensemble, provides a balance and contrast to the solo singing.
Orchestra - used to play the overture (introduction) and to accompany the vocalists and chorus. Use of tremolo and pizzicato.
Oratorio - an unstaged opera, biblical text, performed during the Lenten season. Schütz and Handel are two outstanding composers of oratorios.

G. F. Handel owes his later career success to the oratorio form. His Messiah, which was written in 24 days, is his best known oratorio.

A cantata is similar both in style and format to an oratorio, but was usually based on New Testament subjects.

J. S. Bach often incorporated simple Lutheran hymns into his cantatas. An example is his Cantata No. 140, "Wachet auf" (Wake up).

The concerto became the principal instrumental form of the Baroque. In it, a harpsichord and a chamber orchestra, composed mainly of strings, accompanies a soloist. The standard form for a concerto consists of three movements. The first is moderately fast in tempo, while the second movement is slow. The third movement is usually the fastest in tempo.

Antonio Vivaldi wrote over 500 concertos, with nearly half of them written to feature the violin. Although he was a priest, he pursued a career as a violinist in Venice.

A fugue is a Baroque keyboard form consisting of an exposition, development, recapitulation, and a coda. It uses three or four highly independent parts, imitative counterpoint, a subject, a stretto (imitation in close succession).

Study Questions

1. The Renaissance style, as compared to the Baroque, is:

   a. more reserved
   b. less reserved
   c. about the same
   d. more vocal oriented

2. Which city was important for many musical innovations in the 1600's?

   a. Mantua
   b. Rome
   c. Paris
   d. Venice

3. Which of the following was not an innovation by Gabrieli?

   a. specific instrumentation
   b. development of the fugue
   c. alternating choirs of sound
   d. expression indications

4. The time period for the Baroque is:

    a. 1400 - 1600
    b. 1600 - 1700
    c. 1650 - 1750
    d. 1600 - 1750

5. Music of the Baroque is generally:

    a. instrumental only
    b. vocal only
    c. highly ornate
    d. very reserved

"contend with"

6. The term concertato refers to:

    a. combining vocal and instrumental ensembles
    b. the use of a harpsichord to accompany voices
    c. the elaborate and ornate melodies of the period
    d. none of these

7. The first public opera house was built where?

    a. Rome
    b. Venice
    c. London
    d. Paris

8. Which language was used most frequently for opera singing?

    a. the vernacular
    b. Latin
    c. French
    d. Italian

9. Gabrieli's "In ecclesiis" makes use of:

    a. antiphonal style
    b. concertato principle
    c. alternating choirs and instruments
    d. all of these

10. What most often happens in the B section of an aria?

    a. repeat of the A section
    b. development of the A section
    c. a contrasting section of music
    d. none of these

11. Tremolo is:

a. an orchestral effect
b. a rapid alternation between two notes
c. a device found in the music of Monteverdi
d. all of these

12. Which of the following is not found in an oratorio:

a. scenery
b. soloists
c. keyboard
d. arias

13. An oratorio is:

a. similar to the cantata
b. the same as an opera
c. a new instrumental form
d. both a. and c.

14. In the development section of a fugue, a composer is likely to:

a. develop the main ideas of the exposition
b. exclusively introduce new ideas
c. slow the tempo down
d. repeat the opening exposition

Matching

15. The overall form of a concerto. – 3 part

16. Vivaldi wrote over 500 of them. – concertos

17. Imitative counterpoint is found in this type of music. Fugue

18. The cantata is most similar to this form. Oratorio

19. The ending section of a fugue is called what? Coda

three part
fugue
oratorio
two part
concertos
violin
concertos
coda
stretto
operas

Listening Self-Test

Gabrieli - "In ecclesiis" C.D. No. 1, track 4.

20. This piece is written for:

    a. organ
    b. choir
    c. soloists
    d. all of these

21. Gabrieli keeps changing the:

    a. instrumentation
    b. orchestration
    c. timbres
    d. all of these

22. Voices and instruments perform:

    a. the same music
    b. five verses
    c. five verses and five Alleluia's
    d. a cappella

23. This type of piece is a(n):

    a. motet
    b. oratorio
    c. cantata
    d. opera

24. The final cadence is sung and/or played by:

    a. the voices
    b. the orchestra
    c. the tutti section
    d. the soloists and orchestra

25. One vocal device that Gabrieli uses throughout is:

    a. antiphonal singing
    b. monophonic texture
    c. recitative passages
    d. organum

Handel - "For Unto Us a Child Is Born" from Messiah. C.D. No. 1, track 5.

26. Handel makes extensive use of:

a. the organ
b. costumes and scenery
c. imitation and sequence
d. trumpets and trombones

27. This section is known as a(n):

a. aria
b. chorus
c. recitative
d. mixed ensemble

28. The musical texture alternates between:

a. monophonic and homophonic
b. homophonic and polyphonic
c. monophonic and polyphonic
d. it does not alternate

Bach, J.S., "Wachet auf" from Cantata No. 140. C.D. No. 1, track 6.

29. This piece begins with a(n):

a. recitative
b. chorus
c. fugue
d. instrumental introduction

30. The language of the text is:

a. German
b. Italian
c. Latin
d. French

31. The vocal section that sings Luther's chorale melody first is the:

a. alto
b. soprano
c. tenor
d. bel canto

32. After the melody is sung, the choir then:

a. repeats it exactly
b. changes the music
c. imitates the chorale melody
d. develops the chorale melody

Vivaldi, Concerto for Two Trumpets. C.D. No. 1, track 7.

First Movement

33. The opening motive features:

a. a solo trumpet
b. both trumpets
c. the orchestra only
d. both trumpets and orchestra

34. After the introduction the trumpets:

a. rest
b. play in harmony
c. play one at a time
d. go back to the beginning of the piece

35. The opening motive(s) occur:

a. only at the beginning
b. at the beginning and the end only
c. in both the trumpet and orchestral parts
d. none of the above

36. The key of the piece is:

a. major
b. minor
c. mixed
d. monophonic

Bach, J.S., Brandenburg Concerto No. 2, C.D. No. 1, track 8.
Third Movement

37. The main melody is first played by the:

a. oboe
b. trumpet
c. trumpet and oboe
d. strings

38. The correct order of entrances is:

a. oboe, violin, flute, trumpet
b. violin, oboe, trumpet, harpsichord
c. trumpet, oboe, violin, flute
d. flute, oboe, trumpet, violin

39. Bach uses which device throughout the movement?

a. stretto
b. imitation
c. sectional repetition
d. development

Bach, J.S., Fugue in g minor, C.D. No. 1, track 9.

40. The medium of this work is:

a. piano
b. clavichord
c. organ
d. harpsichord

41. The second entrance is, in relation to the first entrance:

a. higher
b. lower
c. slower
d. in the major

42. How many "voices" are there in this fugue?

a. three
b. four
c. five
d. more than five

43. After all of the voices have entered, Bach begins the:

a. recapitulation
b. coda
c. development
d. counterpoint

Chapter 9. Classical Music

Summary

During this period, the aristocracy continued their demand for more and more music. It was also a time of revolutions and uprisings.
The dates of the Classical Period are approximately 1750 to 1820.

Most French, German, and Austro-Hungarian courts maintained a staff of resident musicians to become a small orchestra to call on for concerts, operas, and dances.

Classical Greek and Roman art influenced architecture, painting, and sculpture. But the term Classical is applied to the music of this period because of the emphasis on clarity of sound and symmetry of form.

Composers of this style include Haydn, Mozart, and the early music of Beethoven. In general, the music is elegant, restrained, balanced and predictable. The forms are clear cut and easy to follow.

Study Questions

1. The political and social development in the Classical period was one of:

   a. complacency
   b. predictability
   (c) revolution
   d. morality

2. Composers in the Classical period were thought of as:

   (a) servants
   b. aristocrats
   c. above the law
   d. equal to the ruling class

3. The duties of the court composer included:

   a. performing
   b. rehearsing the ensemble
   c. writing music
   (d) all of the above

4. Most French and German courts maintained a(n):

   a. orchestra
   b. staff of musicians
   c. court composer
   d. all of the above

5. Classical music was most affected by:

   a. Greek and Roman art
   b. Greek and Roman music
   c. painting and sculpture
   d. none of the above

6. Which composer is not from the Classical period:

   a. Mozart
   b. Haydn
   c. Handel
   d. Beethoven

7. Classical composers were interested in:

   a. balance
   b. symmetry
   c. proportion
   d. all of the above

8. Which large performing medium rose to prominence in this period?

   a. chamber orchestra
   b. symphony orchestra
   c. string ensemble
   d. opera

9. The basic texture of Classical music is:

   a. homophonic
   b. monophonic
   c. diatonic
   d. polyphonic

10. The musical forms of the period are:

   a. long and elaborate
   b. all three part
   c. clear-cut, easy to follow
   d. derived from antiquity

Chapter 10. Music of the Classical Period

Summary

Mozart was a child prodigy who displayed extraordinary musical ability by performing in public on both the violin and piano by the age of four. His legacy includes over 600 compositions in almost every form.

He broke with the tradition of using the Italian language for opera. His operas The Abduction from the Seraglio and The Magic Flute are examples of this.

Haydn - led a more stable life than Mozart. He was a court composer for the Esterhazy family in Hungary and Austria. After the death of his patron, he travelled to London and composed his famous "London" symphonies. He was a mentor and friend of Mozart and a teacher of young Beethoven.

The composer Beethoven studied with Haydn and other composers.

Orchestral and chamber music concerts took place mostly at court. With growing frequency, however, subscription performances were offered in town to the general public.

Composers wrote their works in recognizable forms, and the challenge was to create fresh and interesting works.

Most classical symphonies contain four movements:
I. fast, serious, occasionally it begins with a slow introduction.
II. slow, song-like, melodic.
III. moderately fast, dance-style, like a minuet and trio.
IV. fast, usually the fastest in the symphony. Light and happy in mood.

The concerto features a soloist and orchestra. It generally has three movements:
I. moderately fast, usually with a cadenza (solo section) for the soloist.
II. moderately slow, song-like in style.
III. fast tempo, lively and usually contains a cadenza.

Musical forms can be thought of as musical structure or architecture.

Representative musical forms of this period include:
Sonata form: exposition, development, recapitulation, coda
Minuet and trio form: the outline of the form is a minuet with two themes, followed by a trio with two new themes, then a return to the minuet with its two themes.

Rondo form: main theme recurs after several shorter, contrasting themes.
Theme and variations form: one main theme is used, with a series of variations or modifications following.

Study Questions

1. Which composer was a child prodigy in the Classical period?

   a. Haydn
   b. Doyle
   c. Beethoven
   d. Mozart

2. What was unusual about the opera The Abduction from the Seraglio?

   a. It was in German.
   b. It was a comic opera.
   c. It was performed in Vienna.
   d. none of the above

3. Mozart's legacy does not include:

   a. an opera in English
   b. 27 piano concertos
   c. over 600 compositions
   d. 41 symphonies

4. Ludwig Koechel was:

   a. an attorney
   b. an amateur musician
   c. the cataloger of Mozart's music
   d. all of the above

5. Haydn spent most of his career working for:

   a. the French court
   b. the Esterhazy family
   c. J. P. Salomon
   d. his publisher

6. Orchestra and chamber music concerts took place:

   a. at court
   b. in the church
   c. for the benefit of those in need
   d. for the general public

7. Eighteenth-century concerts consisted mainly of :

a. new music
b. music by living composers
c. music by Baroque composers
d. both a. and b.

8. Most of the music of the period was:

a. hand copied
b. printed and sold
c. available for the general public
d. none of the above

9. Composers wrote music to be:

a. somewhat predictable
b. in recognizable forms
c. performed
d. all of the above

10. The Classical symphony usually has:

a. two movements
b. three movements
c. four movements
d. only one movement

11. The dance-style movement in a symphony is usually:

a. the first movement
b. the third movement
c. the second movement
d. the fourth movement

12. A concerto has:

a. one more movement than a symphony
b. one less movement than a symphony
c. the same amount of movements
d. no separate movements

13. In a rondo form, you will find:

a. a frequent return to the main theme
b. many variations on the main theme
c. several themes and no variations
b. several themes with a series of variations

Piano = classical period or later

14. Don Juan was:

    a. the subject of an opera
    b. a great lover
    c. a Spanish philanderer
    (d) all of the above

Fill in the Blank

15. The second section of the sonata form is called the development.

16. In a typical minuet and trio form there are four (how many) themes.

17. Mozart (composer) broke with tradition and wrote an opera in German.

18. The term singspiel refers to folk theatre.

Listening Self-Test

Mozart, Symphony No. 40. in g minor. C.D. #1, track No. 10.

First Movement - Sonata Allegro Form

19. How would you describe the first theme of the exposition?

    a. stable
    (b) rhythmic
    c. melodic
    d. relaxing

20. What device does the composer use in building his first theme?

    a. imitation
    b. fugue
    (c) sequence
    d. stretto

21. The character of the second theme, in comparison to the first, is more:

    a. rhythmic
    (b). melodic
    c. harmonic
    d. instrumental

22. In the development section, what does Mozart develop?

a. the first theme
b. the second theme
c. both themes
d. new material

23. What is the tempo of this movement?

a. slow
b. moderate
c. fast
d. soft

24. What does Mozart do at the end of the coda to let you know the movement is ending?

a. He goes back to the beginning.
b. He replays the first theme.
c. He makes a cadence.
d. all of the above

Haydn, Symphony No. 94. C. D. No. 1, track 13.

Third Movement

25. What is the form for the third movement?

a. rondo
b. minuet and trio
c. theme and variations
d. sonata form

26. What quality does the third movement possess?

a. dance-like
b. rondo
c. slow and soft
d. melancholy

27. How many different themes are there?

a. two
b. three
c. four
d. more than four

28. A device that Haydn uses when developing the melody is to:

    a. alternate loud and soft
    b. have only the brass play
    c. alternate the full orchestra with a soloist
    d. none of the above

Beethoven, Piano Sonata No. 8, "Pathétique ." C.D. No. 2, track 2.

29. The tempo of the beginning of the movement is:

    a. slow
    b. moderate
    c. very slow
    d. very fast

30. After the first major cadence, Beethoven adds:

    a. an extension
    b. a new melody
    c. a development
    d. silence

31. Theme no. 2 is, compared to theme no. 1:

    a. in the major key
    b. still in minor
    c. goes from p to f
    d. both a. and c.

32. How many times do you hear the transition music between theme 1 and theme 2?

    a. only once
    b. twice
    c. three times
    d. more than three times

33. What happens in the coda?

    a. it gets softer
    b. it stays at the forte level
    c. it crescendos from p to ff
    d. it decrescendos from ff to p

34. Is the coda section a developmental section?

- a. Yes, he develops theme 1.
- b. Yes, he develops theme 2.
- c. No, it is similar to the transition.
- d. No, it is comprised of new material.

Mozart, Piano Concerto No. 21. C.D. No. 1, track 14.

Third Movement

35. How many different themes are there?

- a. two
- b. three
- c. four
- d. only one

36. What is the form of this movement?

- a. rondo
- b. minuet and trio
- c. theme and variations
- d. sonata form

37. How many cadenzas are there?

- a. one
- b. two
- c. three
- d. there are none

38. After theme 4 there is a fermata (held tone). What occurs after the fermata?

- a. a cadence
- b. a cadenza
- c. a crescendo
- d. an accelerando

39. The coda is based on:

- a. theme 1
- b. theme 2
- c. theme 3
- d. new material only

40. The final cadenza is for:

a. strings and piano
b. piano and orchestra
c. woodwinds and piano
d. solo piano

41. At the very end, Mozart ends the concerto with:

a. three loud cadence chords
b. the piano cadenza
c. the minor key
d. the coda and theme 2

Mozart, "Ah, vous dirai je, Maman" C.D. No. 1, track 15.

42. How many different themes are there?

a. one
b. two
c. three
d. more than three

43. What is the form of this movement?

a. rondo
b. minuet and trio
c. theme and variations
d. sonata form

44. What does Mozart change in the first variation?

a. the tempo
b. the melody
c. key to minor
d. all of the above

45. What does Mozart change in the second variation?

a. the key to minor
b. the tempo
c. The melody is in the lower register.
d. The melody is in the upper register.

Mozart, "Catalog Aria" from Don Giovanni. C.D. No. 2, track 1.

46. This piece begins with:

  a. the orchestral introduction
  b. Leporello singing softly
  c. Don Giovanni singing
  d. Donna Elvira crying

47. The piece begins in:

  a. the major key
  b. the minor key
  c. a duple meter
  d. both a. and c.

48. The overall mood of the aria is one of:

  a. sadness
  b. anger
  c. melancholy
  d. humor

Chapter 11. Beethoven: Bridge to Romanticism

Summary

The music of Beethoven became the exemplar for the nineteenth century. His independence became an inspiration for all musicians.

His output was considerable and his influence on future composers was enormous.

Beethoven witnessed the social changes that ultimately resulted in new forms of government, and his music articulates the transition from Classicism to freer forms of the Romantic Period.

His early years were spent in Bonn but he made Vienna his home after the age of 21.

As a child, his father pressured him to emulate Mozart.

After the age of 30, Beethoven was so depressed about his loss of hearing that he wrote what is known as the "Heiligenstadt Testament" expressing his ambivalence about living or dying.

As his music became more personal and powerful, Beethoven demanded more sound from his piano. As a result, pianos were built that were larger and sturdier - similar to today's concert grands.

His Piano Sonata No. 8 is known as the Pathétique Sonata. It was composed in 1799 and shows a tinge of sadness. The form of this rondo is: A - B - A - C - B - A.

As Beethoven searched for a new audience, he took control of his life by organizing and performing in concerts for the middle class. He also sold his works to publishers, as royalties eventually became his main source of income.

There are several noticeable characteristics of his symphonic works - larger forms, more instruments, freer treatment of traditional forms, longer codas and development sections, cyclic treatment of themes, and the connection of movements.

The first movement of his famous Symphony No. 5 is built on a rhythmic motive and has a coda section that is almost as long as any other section in the movement.

The Symphony No. 6 is subtitled the "Pastoral Symphony." In the fourth movement Beethoven creates a full-blown "Thunderstorm."

With the Ninth Symphony Beethoven completely crossed the bridge into Romanticism. For the first time in a symphony, a chorus and vocal soloists performed with the orchestra. In this fourth movement, Beethoven set to music Friedrich Schiller's poem "Ode to Joy." The spirit of the poem is one of universal brotherhood of man.

Study Questions

1. For Beethoven, composing was a(n):

    a. easy task
    b. struggle
    c. only one of his jobs
    d. none of the above

2. Beethoven was born in:

    a. Bonn
    b. Vienna
    c. Paris
    d. London

3. While Haydn wrote over 100 symphonies and Mozart wrote 41, Beethoven only wrote:

    a. 6 symphonies
    b. 9 symphonies
    c. 11 symphonies
    d. 15 symphonies

4. Beethoven's Heiligenstadt Testament was:

    a. an expression of ambivalence towards living or dying
    b. his acceptance of permanent deafness
    c. a letter written to the world to be opened after his death
    d. all of the above

5. Beethoven's search for a more "suitable instrument" led to the development of an instrument similar to today's:

    a. violin
    b. symphony orchestra
    c. organ
    d. piano

6. The form of the third movement from Beethoven's Pathétique Sonata is a:

   a. minuet and trio
   (b.) rondo
   c. theme and variations
   d. sonata

7. Beethoven searched for a:

   a. new patron
   b. new concert hall
   (c.) new audience
   d. none of the above

8. Influenced by the changing social and political structure around him, Beethoven began to:

   a. take control of his own musical life
   b. organize concerts for his own benefit
   c. target the middle class audience
   (d.) all of the above

9. As a composer, Beethoven eventually made what his main source of income?

   a. new commissions
   (b.) royalties
   c. concert promotions
   d. court wages

10. Which of the following is not a characteristic of Beethoven's symphonic works?

   a. freer traditional forms
   b. frequent changes in tempo
   (c.) adherence to Classical formal concepts
   d. use of a larger orchestra

11. Beethoven's Symphony No. 6 is subtitled:

   a. "Heroic"
   (b.) "Pastoral"
   c. "Choral"
   d. "Eroica"

12. While the overall form of the first movement from his Fifth Symphony is classic in design, Beethoven greatly extends the:

a. exposition
b. recapitulation
c. development
d. coda and development

13. Beethoven's "Scene by the Brook" is:

a. a song for voice and piano
b. from his Sixth Symphony
c. an aria from an opera
d. a poem

14. The Sixth Symphony has one more:

a. movement
b. woodwind part
c. development section
d. string section

15. Which work moved Beethoven into the Romantic Period?

a. Pathétique Sonata
b. Ninth Symphony
c. Eroica Symphony
d. Emperor Concerto

16. The spirit behind Schiller's "Ode to Joy" is one of:

a. contentment
b. revolution
c. brotherhood
d. sadness

17. Which symphony of Beethoven's used a chorus and vocal soloists?

a. the Fifth
b. the "Eroica"
c. the "Pastoral"
d. the Ninth

Listening Self-Test

Beethoven, Sonata No. 8, "Pathétique." C. D. No. 2, track 2.
Third Movement

18. The overall mood of the piece:

    a. joyful
    b. sadness
    c. dance-like
    d. frantic

19. Beethoven creates this mood by using:

    a. the major key
    b. the minor key
    c. a large brass section
    d. the string section only

20. The form of this movement is:

    a. A B A C B A
    b. A A B B C C
    c. A B C D E B
    d. A B A A A B

21. The type of form for this movement is called:

    a. sonata
    b. minuet
    c. rondo
    d. theme and variations

Beethoven, Symphony No. 5., C.D. No 2, track 3. First Movement.

22. The opening idea can be called a:

    a. rhythmic motive
    b. melodic motive
    c. harmonic structure
    d. timbre

23. After the beginning of the piece, Beethoven continues to:

    a. start and stop
    b. sequence the idea
    c. repeat the first theme idea
    d. all of the above

24. In contrast to the first theme, the second theme is more:

a. rhythmic
b. percussive
c. melodic
d. developmental

25. At the end of the exposition, Beethoven goes directly into:

a. the development
b. the recapitulation
c. a repeat of the exposition
d. none of the above

26. The development section is based on:

a. the first theme
b. the second theme
c. new material
d. the coda

27. In the recapitulation, Beethoven adds:

a. a fourth horn part
b. an oboe solo
c. a string cadenza
b. more percussion

28. The coda section actually becomes:

a. a second development section
b. almost as long as the recapitulation
c. equal in importance to the other three sections
d. all of the above

Beethoven, Symphony No. 6. C.D. No. 2, track 4.

Fourth Movement

29. This movement is a musical:

a. dance scene
b. thunderstorm
c. scene by a brook
d. sonata-allegro form

30. At the end of the movement, Beethoven has the musical description:

a. crescendo and move closer
b. decrescendo and move into the distance
c. maintain its fury
d. none of the above

Chapter 12. The Romantic Period

Summary

After 1820, Romanticism became the predominant style in all the arts.

It reflected a new concern with emotional expression.
Composers no longer had to defer to patrons.
Excess and exuberance often led to pessimism and depression.

It was during this period that many of the great cultural centers were born, including Paris, Vienna, Prague, and London. Public concerts, opera and ballet companies were established throughout Europe and the United States. Artists became members of the privileged class and were no longer merely servants.

Favorite subjects of the Romantic artists included the supernatural, the exotic, nature, and love and death.

In trying to find new ways to communicate with an audience, composers offered new ideas in the titles and stories of their music. This was the beginning of Program Music. Romantic music gives us an opportunity to experience our feelings.

The general characteristics of Romantic music: emotional, subjective, large ensembles, extra-musical ideas (program music), rubato, complex rhythms and changing tempi, long melodies, complex harmonies, full range of dynamics, mainly homophonic texture but with polyphonic development sections. While there is a continued use of Classical period forms, many new types are developed (tone poem, art song, etc.).

Study Questions

1. The Romantic period began approximately around:

   a. 1750
   b. 1780
   c. 1820
   d. 1870

2. The Romantic spirit can be found in:

   a. art
   b. music
   c. theater
   d. all of the arts

3. In the Romantic period artists no longer had to rely upon:

   a. a patron
   b. the church
   c. the aristocracy
   (d.) all of the above

4. Paris, Vienna, Budapest, Dresden and Leipzig were all:

   a. centers of major opera companies
   b. cities where ballet began
   (c.) emerging cultural centers of the world
   d. major centers of industry

5. Nature, beauty, magic, and the mystic are all:

   a. subjects of Beethoven's opera Don Giovanni
   (b.) favorite subjects of Romantic artists
   c. subjects that were banned by the aristocracy
   d. both a. and c.

6. In general, Romantic music is:

   (a.) more expressive than Classical music
   b. less expressive than Classical music
   c. similar to Baroque
   d. none of the above

7. Romantic composers became fascinated with:

   a. the possibilities of emotional expression
   b. the use of expanded musical elements
   c. the use of instrumental tone colors
   (d.) all of the above

Matching

8. Pushkin, Poe, and Whitman are all: writers
9. Music that has extra-musical connotations. program music
10. Romantic melodies, as compared to Classical melodies, are more what? emotional
11. Which of these is not a Romantic form? fugue

composers
absolute music
program music
artists
fugue
emotional
restrained
nocturne
writers
art song

Chapter 13. Early Romantic Music

Summary

The life of Hector Berlioz typifies the spirit of the Romantic period. Although he had no formal musical training as a child, after studying music in Paris and Italy he eventually became one of the world's great composers.

Berlioz is known for his ability to orchestrate - to combine and score instruments in a unique manner. He wrote the first important textbook on orchestration.

Berlioz was always interested in the dramatic possibilities of music as his *Symphonie Fantastique* demonstrates. Central to this work is the idée fixe or the fixed idea. This idea is a musical representation of Harriet Smithson, the actress Berlioz became infatuated with.

In order to create various moods, Berlioz calls for the string performers to play with mutes (con sordino) and to produce eerie, glassy sounds (sul ponticello). To simulate dancing skeletons the performers turn their bows around and strike the strings with the wood of the bow (col legno battutta).

In writing the fifth movement, "Dream of a Witches' Sabbath," Berlioz uses a sectional form.

Franz Schubert, another Romantic composer, is known for his development of the art song - a piece for voice and piano. Schubert was the first composer to raise the pianist to the level of an equal partner with the voice. In German, the art song is known as the *lieder*.

In Schubert's "The Erlking" notice how the piano creates the mood of a galloping horse and how the vocalist is asked to sing four different characters - the narrator, the ill child, the father on horseback, and the Erlking (death). The subject, death and the supernatural, are typically Romantic.

Robert Schumann is another composer of art songs. He was not only a piano prodigy but also a writer and editor for "Zeitschrift für Musik" (The New Journal for Music). His wife, Clara, was also a gifted pianist and his song "Widmung" (Dedication) was written for her and performed at their wedding.

Frédéric Chopin was born Warsaw, Poland and settled in Vienna where he spent the remainder of his life. Chopin was one of the greatest composers of piano music and preferred to perform for small audiences in salon concerts.

Franz Liszt, another composer of piano music, was also known for his great piano virtuosity. He, along with Chopin, developed a variety of simple, intimate forms for the piano; i.e., ballades, fantasies, nocturnes, etc.

Felix Mendelssohn's musical talents were often compared with Mozart's. Traveling extensively throughout Germany, England, Scotland, and Italy, Mendelssohn incorporated his impressions of these countries into musical compositions. Mendelssohn assembled concert programs similar to what we find today - works by several composers from different style periods.

Study Questions

1. As a musician, Berlioz was most skilled at playing:

    a. the piano
    b. the violin
    c. the cello and guitar
    d. no particular instrument

2. As a writer, Berlioz wrote the first important treatise on:

    a. composing
    b. orchestration
    c. piano performance
    d. string instruments

3. Berlioz spent most of his life in which cultural center?

    a. Vienna
    b. Dresden
    c. Paris
    d. Bonn

4. The central theme to the Symphonie Fantastique is called:

    a. the principal idea
    b. the idée fixe
    c. the leitmotif
    d. the program

5. The <u>Symphonie Fantastique</u> is written about his:

   a. dreams of fame and fortune
   b. musical aspirations
   c. love for his country
   d. obsession with an actress

6. The "Dream of a Witches' Sabbath" uses which Gregorian chant?

   a. Idée Fixe
   b. Dies Irae
   c. Con sordino
   d. Sul ponticello

7. Romantic music that tells a story is known as:

   a. program music
   b. absolute music
   c. ideal music
   d. chamber music

8. Schubert wrote:

   a. piano music
   b. art songs
   c. symphonies
   d. all of the above

9. "The Erlking" is a(n):

   a. art song
   b. German lieder
   c. concerto
   d. both a. and b.

10. Which composer raised the piano to the same level as the voice?

   a. Schumann
   b. Beethoven
   c. Chopin
   d. Schubert

11. Which character in "The Erlking" represents death?

   a. the father
   b. the child
   c. the Erlking
   d. the narrator

12. Salon concerts were held in the :

a. homes of wealthy music enthusiasts
b. courts of wealthy aristocrats
c. church
d. large concert halls throughout Europe

13. The popularity of the piano and piano music encouraged composers to:

a. publish their music
b. perform for friends
c. hold classes on piano performance
d. none of the above

14. The term Impromptu suggests:

a. that the pianist must be able to improvise
b. that the pianist is free to improvise
c. a feeling of spontaneity
d. the piece is entirely improvised

15. Which Romantic composer was compared with Mozart?

a. Berlioz
b. Schubert
c. Chopin
d. Mendelssohn

16. Mendelssohn was important for:

a. programming the music of living composers
b. programming only his own music
c. programming the music of composers from several style periods
d. teaching other composers how to write musical criticism

17. Inspired by Beethoven's Piano Concerto No. 2, Mendelssohn indicates:

a. the cadenza to be played by the soloist
b. the dynamics of the orchestra accompanying the soloist
c. where the soloist is free to improvise
d. no stops between movements

Fill in the Blank

18. What does Schubert use to represent the horse in "The Erlking?" the ____________ .

19. Name the composer who was also a writer for an important German music journal. ____________ ________________ .

20. "Widmung" was written for _______ _______________ .

21. The composer who was known for writing hundreds of pieces in a variety of short forms known as intimate piano pieces was ___________ .

22. Perhaps the greatest pianist of the nineteenth century was ____________ .

Listening Self-Test

Berlioz, "Dream of a Witches' Sabbath" from <u>Symphonie Fantastique</u>. C.D. No. 2, track 5.

Fifth Movement

23. The form of this movement relies upon:

    a. sectional form
    b. imitation
    c. stretto
    d. both b. and c.

24. This movement uses which string technique(s)?

    a. sul ponticello
    b. con sordino
    c. col legno battuta
    d. all of the above

25. The Dies Irae is introduced by which instruments?

    a. trombones and percussion
    b. trombones and tuba
    c. trumpets and trombones
    d. horns and trumpets

26. After the Dies Irae, Berlioz creates a loosely constructed:

a. form
b. fugue
c. stretto
d. recapitulation

Schubert, "The Erlking" Art Song. C.D. No. 2, track 6.

27. This piece is known as:

a. an art song
b. German lieder
c. a tone poem
d. both a. and b.

28. While there are four characters:

a. there is only one vocalist
b. there are two vocalists
c. there is one voice and the piano
d. there are three vocalists

29. The text for this piece was written by:

a. Schubert
b. Dudevant
c. Goethe
d. Schiller

30. At the beginning, the piano represents:

a. the Erlking
b. death
c. life and hope
d. a galloping horse

31. At the end of the piece:

a. the Erlking gives up
b. the father saves the boy
c. the boy is taken by the Erlking
d. the horse dies

Schumann, "Widmung" Art Song. C.D. No. 3, track 7.

32. The text was written by:

a. Clara Schumann
b. Robert Schumann
c. Franklin Heuser
d. Friedrich Ruckert

33. The mood of the piece starts out:

a. calm
b. excited
c. angry
d. soft

34. After the singer finishes, Schumann quotes:

a. Schubert's "Ave Maria"
b. Schubert's "The Erlking"
c. Chopin's "Fantaisie-Impromptu"
d. Schumann's Piano Concerto No. 1

Chopin, Fantaisie-Impromptu Op. 66. C. D. No. 2, track 8.

35. This piece is known as a(n):

a. art song
b. improvised piano work
c. intimate piano piece
d. tone poem

36. The mood and expression of the piece has a(n):

a. wide range
b. narrow sense
c. introspective quality
d. calm and serene quality

37. The deviations from the steady tempo are known as:

a. timbre
b. leitmotif
c. rubato
d. crescendo

Mendelssohn, <u>Violin Concerto in e minor</u>. C.D. No. 2, track 9.

First Movement

38. At the beginning of the piece:

    a. the violinist has to wait a long time before entering
    b. the orchestra plays the main theme
    c. the violinist enters almost immediately with the main theme
    d. none of the above

39. An outstanding feature of this movement is the:

    a. use of lyrical melodies
    b. use of brass to play the melodies
    c. innovative use of percussion
    d. use of several cadenzas

40. Mendelssohn did not:

    a. care if the performer improvised his cadenza
    b. allow the performer to improvise
    c. write any cadenzas in the first movement
    d. write any cadenzas in the entire concerto

Chapter 14. Romantic Opera

Summary

Opera is dramatized music. It includes sung dialogue, costumes and scenery, a cast of characters, dancing, and an orchestra for accompaniment. Opera became a popular medium for nineteenth century Romantic composers and audiences. Early opera was primarily a series of songs.

With grand opera, all the subjects, spirit, and extra-musical ideas associated with Romanticism materialized in the grandest manner.

Opera stars are often virtuoso performers who were called upon to act and were given quality stories by the Romantic composers.

Italian composers and the Italian language dominated opera from 1600 into the early Romantic period. Rossini, Donizetti, and Bellini created a new round of exciting Italian operas.

The bel canto (beautiful singing) style characterized early Italian opera. Rossini built a reputation throughout Italy as a brilliant opera composer. Donizetti, one of the most prolific of all opera composers, became famous for his dazzling arias which are extremely difficult to sing. Bellini's ten operas brought him great success and fame before his death at the age of 33. Like Bellini, he wrote in both Italian and French.

Giuseppe Verdi and Richard Wagner are both credited with developing opera into a fully integrated art form. Verdi's innovations include the use of a high quality libretto, believable characters, arias blended into the dramatic action, and expressive orchestral interludes and accompaniments.

Few composers have had as great a gift for composing soaring, emotional melodies as Giacomo Puccini. Many of his operas are tragic love stories set far from Italy. His opera La Bohème (The Bohemian Life) uses verismo or the realistic style of opera. It is based on a novel and in typical verismo style, La Bohème takes a romantic approach to the struggle of artists and common workers.

During the first half of the nineteenth century Paris became an important cultural center. Composers of all nations flocked to Paris to have their works performed. There were three distinct styles of opera in France - grand opera, comic opera, and lyric opera. Grand opera emphasized the spectacle, comic opera emphasized wit and satire, while lyric opera's main appeal was in its melodies and romantic stories.

One of the most popular operas in music, Carmen, was written by the Parisian Georges Bizet. With its focus on two passionate lovers and Carmen's realistic death in Seville's square, it began a trend of operatic realism (verismo).

Nowhere in Europe was the bonding between music and literature as strong as in Germany. Imbued with the ideals of Romanticism, German composers sought out librettos incorporating many Romantic ideals. While Carl Maria von Weber achieved success with his opera Der Freischütz (The Freeshooter), it was Richard Wagner who carried Romantic opera to its extreme.

Wagner's vision was to create a total art work (Gesamtkunstwerk) which he called music drama. He wrote the librettos, composed and orchestrated the music, designed the sets and staging, and conducted the music. He even had his own opera house built in Bayreuth.

Since many of his operas are long, some lasting up to five hours, Wagner used specific musical devices to represent particular characters or ideas. This process is called the leitmotif. It is similar to what Hector Berlioz did to represent Harriet in the Symphonie Fantastique.

Wagner's opera Die Meistersinger von Nürenberg (The Mastersingers of Nuremberg) displays the relationship between the creative artist and the critics, as well as the conflict between tradition and innovation. The opera is set in sixteenth-century Nuremberg (Germany) when the craft guilds (professional unions) were at their high point. The overture to the opera acquaints the audience with the main melodies (leitmotifs) and sets the mood for the story.

Study Questions

1. Opera is:

   a. sung dialogue
   b. elaborate costumes
   c. scenery and music
   d. dramatized music

2. By adding singers and a text in his Ninth Symphony, Beethoven was able to:

   a. push the limits of vocal music
   b. incorporate opera into the symphony
   c. say more than instrumental music alone could
   d. both a. and b.

3. In early operas, when it was time for an aria:

   a. often all the action stopped
   b. the orchestra stopped playing
   c. the audience would applaud
   d. none of the above

4. Which language dominated the librettos until the Romantic period?

   a. French
   b. German
   c. Italian
   d. English

5. The bel canto style of singing refers to:

   a. the style found in early Italian opera
   b. beautiful singing
   c. both a. and b.
   d. none of the above

6. Which composer is not from the Italian tradition?

   a. Bellini
   b. Rossini
   c. Verdi
   d. Weber

7. The stories of <u>Madame Butterfly</u> and <u>Turandot</u> are set:

   a. in Italy
   b. in France
   c. far away from Italy
   d. in German

8. The opera <u>La Bohème</u> uses which style?

   a. verismo
   b. bel canto
   c. grand opera
   d. opera comique

9. The story of <u>La Bohème</u> centers around:

   a. Parisian aristocrats
   b. Parisian artists
   c. Parisian artists and common workers
   d. both a. and b.

10. Which item below did not contribute to the development of Paris into a major cultural center?

   a. the French Revolution
   b. the turbulence of the Napoleonic Empire
   c. the rising middle class
   d. the industrial revolution

11. Grand opera emphasized:

   a. verismo
   b. spectacle
   c. comedy
   d. lyric melodies

12. Which composer wrote the opera Carmen?

   a. Bizet
   b. Gounod
   c. Wagner
   d. Verdi

13. Wagner's goal was to:

   a. write operas in the Italian tradition
   b. create a total art work
   c. exert total control over every aspect of his operas
   d. both b. and c.

Matching

14. In his music dramas, Wagner used which device to link the music to the story?

15. The relationships between creative artists and their critics is the subject of which Wagnerian music drama?

16. Gilbert and Sullivan were writers of ?

17. Carmen is an example of which type of opera?

Parsifal
overture
Meistersinger
verismo
opera
comedy
fixed idea
Rienzi
leitmotif
operetta

Listening Self-Test

Puccini, La Bohème. "Che gelida manina!" C.D. No. 3, track 1.

18. The story centers around:

    a. artists in Bohemia
    b. artists of the Left Bank in Paris
    c. Rudolfo and Mimi
    d. both b. and c.

19. The apartment is cold because:

    a. they have just arrived
    b. they cannot afford to pay for the fuel
    c. they have forgotten to pay their bills
    d. the landlord has turned off the gas

20. What Rudolfo sings to Mimi is called a(n):

    a. verismo
    b. recitative
    c. aria
    d. soliloquy

21. As they leave the stage, they are singing:

    a. about their love for one another
    b. a duet
    c. about the fulfillment of their dreams
    d. all of the above

Wagner, Overture to Die Meistersinger von Nürenberg. C.D. No. 2, track 10.

22. How many main melodies, leitmotifs, are found in the overture?

    a. two
    b. three
    c. four
    d. five

23. Which instruments does he use to represent the love theme first?

    a. flute and piano
    b. flute and then the oboe
    c. oboe and violin
    d. the full orchestra

24. To create the feeling of power, Wagner uses which orchestral section?

a. the strings
b. the woodwinds
c. the percussion
d. the brass

25. The first leitmotif represents:

a. the medieval German burgher
b. nobility and dependability
c. the Mastersingers
d. all of the above

Chapter 15. Late Romantic Music

Summary

By the second half of the nineteenth century professional composers had become highly respected and financially secure. Public concert societies assumed the task of promoting and staging concerts.

Mainstream concert music split into two camps - Wagner championed the radical movement while Brahms the traditional movement.

Wagner and his followers favored a wandering tonality, conveying the feeling of an extended journey. Much of the music is programmatic and built around stories or descriptive titles.

Brahms still adhered to the classical traditions of Haydn, Mozart, Schubert and Beethoven. Both Schumann and Brahms focused their attention on chamber music.

Unlike Beethoven, Brahms was not an innovator but more of a renovator. He labored over his own first symphony for 20 years. In appreciation for being honored as "Germany's leading composer," Brahms wrote the Academic Festival Overture in 1880. It is a "very boisterous potpourri of student songs."

As wealthy art patrons opened their homes to musicians, more and more chamber music was written for these performances. The setting for chamber music is much more intimate and watching the musicians is an integral part of enjoying the music.

Gustav Mahler and Richard Strauss were two outstanding composer-conductors. Mahler's demanding perfectionism earned him a reputation as a tyrant. His symphonies abound with extra-musical references such as poetry and philosophy. His Third Symphony lasts one hour and thirty-five minutes and his Eighth Symphony calls for over one thousand performers.

Mahler's first symphony is subtitled "The Titan" and has some similarities with Beethoven's <u>Pastoral Symphony</u>. In this work, he uses a highly flexible and complex form that relies heavily on melodic ideas for continuity.

Late nineteenth century composers carried the ideas of program music to the extreme. The term program music describes music that contains a story or text upon which the music is based. Of all the programmatic composers, Richard Strauss was the most successful in merging a program with music.

His works are called tone poems or symphonic poems. An example of a tone poem is his work Don Juan - the same character who inspired Mozart's Don Giovanni.

Study Questions

1. Who or what was responsible for promoting concerts?

   a. composers
   b. agents
   c. concert societies
   d. both a. and b.

2. Wagner championed the:

   a. radical movement
   b. traditional movement
   c. Brahmsians
   d. none of the above

3. In the music of the radicals, formal control gave way to:

   a. restraint
   b. emotion
   c. traditionalism
   d. absolute music

4. The Academic Festival Overture is a collection of:

   a. drinking songs
   b. student songs
   c. religious melodies
   d. both a. and b.

5. Which ensemble is not a chamber ensemble?

   a. symphony orchestra
   b. piano trio
   c. piano quartet
   d. string quartet

6. Which two composers continued in the composer-conductor tradition of Mendelssohn?

   a. Berlioz and Brahms
   b. Strauss and Brahms
   c. Mahler and Strauss
   d. Schubert and Schumann

7. Mahler's First Symphony is patterned after:

   a. Beethoven's Fifth Symphony
   b. Beethoven's Sixth Symphony
   c. Berlioz's Symphonie Fantastique
   d. Strauss's Don Juan

8. As a theme, Mahler borrows musical material from his:

   a. art songs
   b. "Songs of a Wayfarer"
   c. Beethoven's Sixth Symphony
   d. "Symphony of a Thousand"

9. Late Romantic program music is characterized by:

   a. the development of the tone poem
   b. the reliance on a program for an account of the action
   c. a movement towards traditional forms
   d. both a. and b.

Fill in the Blank

10. Mahler's First Symphony is subtitled the ____________ .

11. Mahler sought psychological advice from ____________ .

12. The instrument that Richard Strauss wrote two great concertos for was the ____________ .

13. _________ (a composer) did not adhere to the classical traditions.

14. The music of Brahms is most similar to the music of __________ .

Listening Self-Test

Brahms, Academic Festival Overture, C.D. No. 3, track 2.

15. The piece begins at which dynamic level?

   a. pp
   b. mf
   c. f
   d. fff

16. The meter at the beginning is:

    a. duple
    b. triple
    c. mixed
    d. none of the above

17. How many themes are used in the overture?

    a. only one
    b. two
    c. five
    d. seven or more

18. The mood at the end of the piece is one of:

    a. sadness
    b. tenderness
    c. triumph
    d. eeriness

Brahms, Trio in E-Flat, Op. 40. C.D. No. 2, track 11.

Third Movement

19. The overall form of the movement is:

    a. Classical in design
    b. sonata form
    c. exposition, development, recap, and coda
    d. all of the above

20. The first theme is played by the:

    a. violin
    b. violin with piano accompaniment
    c. horn
    d. piano alone

21. The second theme is first introduced by the:

    a. piano
    b. violin
    c. horn
    d. all of the above

22. In the development section, Brahms develops which theme(s)?

a. theme one
b. theme one and two
c. theme two
d. he uses new material exclusively

Mahler, Symphony No. 1, "The Titan." C.D. No. 3, track 3.

First Movement

23. In the introduction, what effect is Mahler after?

a. the sounds of the city
b. the sounds of nature
c. the sounds of the forest
d. the sounds of the ocean

24. Which instruments play the first two fanfares?

a. the clarinets and strings
b. the strings and brass
c. the off-stage trumpets and clarinets
d. the flutes and clarinets

25. When Mahler introduces the Forest Melody, which instruments play it?

a. the horns
b. the trumpets
c. the strings
d. the woodwinds

26. How often do the mood and the tempo change?

a. they don't
b. rarely
c. occasionally
d. frequently

Chapter 16. Nationalism

Summary

Nationalism is an intense awareness of national identity. It ignited parts of Europe, Scandinavia and Russia throughout the nineteenth century. It seems to have coincided with the American and French Revolutions. With the people demanding a greater role in their governments, clusters of cities and states consolidated.

Another contributing factor to the growing nationalistic movement was the Industrial Revolution. Increased travel and modes of transportation allowed artists to explore the world and then incorporate their discoveries into their art. As nationalism gained momentum, composers in many countries began to examine their own people and folk culture.

The "Russian Five" incorporated situations from history, folklore, legend, and native instruments into their music. They include Mussorgsky, Rimsky-Korsakov, Cui, Balakirev, and Borodin.

Searching for a new Russian musical language, Mussorgsky became fascinated with the spoken language of Russia. He incorporated its unique flavor into his songs and operas.

Based on the text by Alexander Pushkin is Mussorgsky's opera Boris Godunov. While the "Coronation Scene" begins with the sounding of the great bells of Moscow, Mussorgsky also incorporates Russian folk songs and church hymns.

As a nationalist, the Russian Five excluded Tchaikovsky because he did not consistently display the constant nationalistic fervor that they did. Tchaikovsky was considered to be too cosmopolitan. Many of his works, however, contain Russian folk songs and his 1812 Overture epitomizes his passion as a Russian nationalist. It was written to celebrate the 70th anniversary of Napoleon's defeat in Moscow and his subsequent retreat to Paris. The work opens with a Russian hymn, uses cannons and rifle sounds, and fragments of the French national anthem.

Of the twentieth-century Russian composers, Scriabin and Rachmaninov show two different tendencies. Scriabin was a modernist while Rachmaninov, in contrast, remained a Romanticist.

In other parts of the world, the composers Dvorák, Liszt, Bartók, Sibelius, Grieg, Elgar, Vaughan Williams, Grainger, Respighi, de Falla, Albéniz, all show some nationalistic tendencies.

Study Questions

1. Nationalism in music can include:

   a. the use of folk music
   b. the use of folk lore or legend
   c. both a. and b.
   d. none of the above

2. In addition to the Industrial Revolution, what else affected nationalism?

   a. travel
   b. the formation of cities
   c. incorporating discoveries into art forms
   d. all of the above

3. Since the time of Vivaldi and Bach, which music had dominated the Western world?

   a. German music
   b. French, German and Italian music
   c. Italian opera
   d. Classical music

4. The musical training of the Russian Five was:

   a. extensive formal training
   b. imported from the West
   c. very little formal training
   c. both a. and b.

5. Which composer was not a member of the Russian Five?

   a. Mussorgsky
   b. Tchaikovsky
   c. Cui
   d. Borodin

6. The "Coronation Scene" from Boris Godunov begins with:

   a. the vocalist
   b. the orchestra
   c. a Russian hymn
   d. the bells of Russia

7. The character Boris is one of the few lead roles written for:

   a. a male
   b. a tenor
   c. a bass
   d. a baritone

8. The composer of Swan Lake and the Nutcracker is:

   a. Berlioz
   b. Tchaikovsky
   c. Rimsky-Korsakov
   d. Vaughan Williams

9. The 1812 Overture depicts the:

   a. victory of the Russian army over Napoleon
   b. the retreat of Napoleon back to Paris
   c. battle between the Russian and French by using folk music
   d. all of the above

10. The most well-known works of Rimsky-Korsakov are his:

    a. symphonies
    b. art songs and operas
    c. symphonic poems and operas
    d. piano and violin concertos

11. In comparison with Rachmaninov, Scriabin is:

    a. more conservative
    b. more modern
    c. more Romantic
    d. none of the above

12. Which composer is not a representative of Hungarian Nationalism?

    a. Liszt
    b. Bartók
    c. Kodály
    d. Grainger

13. Which Italian composer is not considered a Nationalist?

    a. Verdi
    b. Puccini
    c. Respighi
    d. Donizetti

Listening Self-Test

Mussorgsky, Boris Godunov, "Coronation Scene." C. D. No. 3, track 4.

14. The bells at the beginning of the scene:

    a. represent victory in battle
    b. signify the beginning of the Revolution
    c. are used for dramatic effect
    d. ring very softly, off in the distance

15. The fanfares that enter before the "Toast" are played by:

    a. the full orchestra
    b. the trumpets
    c. the woodwinds
    d. the percussion

16. When the chorus enters, they sing what?

    a. a sad funeral song
    b. a Russian folk song
    c. the main theme sung by Boris
    d. none of the above

17. How does Mussorgsky let you know that Boris is sad during his monologue?

    a. by the text
    b. by the shifting tonalities
    c. by the brooding melody in minor
    d. all of the above

18. Just before the final cadence, a Russian Folk Song is:

    a. played by the orchestra
    b. sung by Boris
    c. sung and played by both chorus and orchestra
    d. sung by the men in the choir only

Tchaikovsky, 1812 Overture, C.D. No. 3, track 5.

19. The very beginning of the piece is a:

    a. Russian folk song
    b. Russian drinking song
    c. Russian Church hymn
    d. not a Russian theme at all

20. The second theme of the piece is:

    a. a Russian folk song
    b. similar to the first theme
    c. the French National Anthem
    d. none of the above

21. What musical technique(s) does Tchaikovsky use when the "Marseillaise" theme is introduced?

    a. imitation
    b. sequence
    c. shifting tonalities
    d. all of the above

22. Another Russian Folk Song in the piece is the:

    a. lullaby
    b. folk dance
    c. both a. and b.
    d. none of these

23. The final theme is the:

    a. Marseillaise
    b. Czar's theme
    c. folk dance
    d. Church hymn

Chapter 17. Impressionism

Summary

Alienated by German intellectualism and Romantic oversentimentality, French artists began to create quieter, more sensual artistic expressions.

French painters, who sought to create an impression of an object rather than its detailed and specific content, began this style known as Impressionism.
The works of Monet, Manet, and Renoir are representative of this style.

Two inventions helped these artists - the camera and the paint tube. Artists were no longer limited to making pencil sketches of their outdoor subjects.
Monet began his life-long fascination with the changing patterns of light, shadow, and color on lily pads in his pond. The movement in music was championed by Claude Debussy.

Taking a cue from Monet, Debussy used the orchestra not for its power and drama, but for the possibilities of its color and combinations of color. Debussy avoided clear-cut cadences, used delicate tone colors (flute, oboes, muted strings, harp), and called for vague rhythms in his music. He also incorporated nontraditional scales that he had been exposed to at the Paris World Expositions. These include the pentatonic, chromatic, and whole-tone scales.

Debussy also added more notes to the traditional chords in an attempt to blur, or less clearly define, the key center.

Maurice Ravel was another French Impressionistic composer. Like Debussy, he also studied at the Paris conservatory. Ravel composed in many styles and may have inspired Gershwin to write his <u>An American in Paris</u> as a result of their discussions about jazz.

Study Questions

1. Impressionistic art tends to:

    a. be vague in definition
    b. use uncomplicated subject matter
    c. be portrayed in pastel colors
    d. all of the above

2. Until the invention of the camera, painters often earned their living by:

   a. painting portraits
   b. painting for the aristocracy
   c. painting for the church
   d. all of the above

3. The invention of the paint tube allowed the artist:

   a. to have more colors at his disposal
   b. to have the paint become absorbed more quickly
   c. the freedom to paint outdoors
   d. none of the above

4. The music of Debussy was:

   a. influenced by Impressionistic art
   b. similar to the music of Wagner
   c. the same tradition as Brahms
   d. the spirit of Russian Nationalism

5. Which of these instruments does Debussy use sparingly?

   a. flutes
   b. oboes
   c. clarinets
   d. brass

6. The purpose of using nontraditional scales is:

   a. to capture the exotic
   b. to use new musical resources
   c. to sound less Germanic
   d. all of the above

7. Pentatonic scales are found in:

   a. native-American songs
   b. folk songs
   c. the music of Beethoven
   d. both a. and b.

Matching

8. This scale is a nontraditional scale.

9. With regards to harmony, Debussy tends to do what?

10. Who was the poet that inspired the Prelude to the Afternoon of a Faun?

11. The other French composer who embraced Impressionism was?

Ravel
diatonic
simplify
Mallarme
Miller
Jannequin
extend
Respighi
whole-tone
Roher

Listening Self-Test

Debussy, Prelude to the Afternoon of a Faun, C.D. No. 3, track 6.

12. Which instrument opens and closes the piece?

a. harp
b. oboe
c. muted strings
d. flute

13. The scale that is played by the instrument in Question #12 is:

a. traditional
b. chromatic
c. whole-tone
d. both a. and c.

14. Another less common instrument that is used very colorfully is the:

a. trumpet
b. harp
c. cello
d. trombone

15. The overall mood of the piece is:

a. dreamy
b. tense
c. dark and stormy
d. romance

Chapter 18. The Twentieth Century Style

Summary

The influence of the two World Wars on Europe was enormous. Many of the libraries, theater, and museums lay in ruins and economies were in shambles.

As for the arts, the European artistic community was devastated. Searching for new ways to express the upheaval of their turbulent times, musicians and artists sought new forms of expression.

The invention of new musical languages and the continued breaking with tradition created a huge gap between composers and audiences. Art, it seemed, no longer had to be beautiful or uplift the spirit. During the present period, the definition of art has come to be redefined.

In general, the music often sounds dissonant and complex. There is a tendency to be experimental. Computer generated sounds and the tape recorder have become important musical resources. Rhythm, melody and harmony are expanded and new musical forms are also developed.

Study Questions

1. In addition to expanding musical resources, avant-garde composers have:

   a. returned to traditional values
   b. invented new musical languages
   c. followed in the footsteps of Wagner
   d. none of the above

2. Instead of creating a vehicle for beautiful sounds, composers thought music to be:

   a. more cerebral
   b. less sensory
   c. a thought-provoking exercise
   d. all of the above

3. Another word for chance music is:

   a. absolute music
   b. aleatoric music
   c. electronic music
   d. none of the above

4. Musique concrète is:

   a. traditional sounds recorded on tape and manipulated
   b. environmental sounds recorded on tape and manipulated
   c. the new musical language used by Stravinsky
   d. both a. and b.

5. Chance music is:

   a. improvised
   b. in the control of the performer
   c. less predictable
   d. all of the above

6. In general, the music of the twentieth century is:

   a. more complex
   b. more dissonant
   c. less asymmetrical
   d. both a. and b.

7. In terms of performing media, which group is used more often?

   a. symphony orchestra
   b. philharmonic orchestra
   c. chamber orchestra
   d. none of the above

8. Which of the following is not a twentieth century rhythmic trend?

   a. polytext
   b. polyrhythm
   c. irregular patterns
   d. polymeter

9. New forms of music in this period include:

   a. musique concrète
   b. electronic music
   c. computer music
   d. all of the above

10. The forms of this period tend to be more:

   a. rational
   b. experimental
   c. traditional
   d. objective

Chapter 19. Stravinsky: Into the Twentieth Century

Summary

Stravinsky held a position similar to Beethoven's a century earlier. Today, Stravinsky looms as one of the most dominant musical forces of the twentieth century. His work The Rite of Spring is a landmark musical composition.

Stravinsky came to prominence after being commissioned by the director of the Ballet Russes (Russian Ballet), Diaghilev, to write the music for his Firebird. A year later followed the successful ballet Petrushka.

In 1913 the Ballet Russes premiered The Rite of Spring in Paris. It was subtitled "Scenes from Pagan Russia." The work is divided into two parts. Part One is "The Adoration of the Earth" and Part Two is entitled "The Sacrifice." Unfamiliar with Stravinsky's new musical language, the premier caused a riot.

This new musical language includes the techniques of polychords, polytonality, polyrhythms, and polymeters. These result from the superimposition of two or more coherent ideas on top of each other. This is called musical double-exposure.

Other devices include the use of irregular metrical patterns, changing metrical patterns, and ostinato.

Study Questions

1. Of Stravinsky's early works, which one was the most controversial?

    a. Firebird
    b. Petrushka
    c. Fireworks
    d. Rite of Spring

2. Picasso and Braque created a new art technique around 1910 called:

    a. expressionism
    b. abstraction
    c. cubism
    d. primitivism

3. A polychord is:

   a. two or more triads performed simultaneously
   b. two or more keys performed simultaneously
   c. several incoherent ideas stacked on top of each other
   d. none of the above

4. Changing metrical patterns creates a feeling of:

   a. calm
   b. sadness
   c. unpredictability
   d. stability

5. An ostinato is:

   a. a tone color procedure
   b. a harmonic device
   c. inspired by African rhythms
   d. a shift in tonal centers

6. The Rite of Spring was premiered in which city?

   a. Moscow
   b. Paris
   c. Rome
   d. London

Listening Self-Test

Stravinsky, The Rite of Spring, "Sacrificial Dance." C.D. No. 4, track 1.

7. This music relies heavily on:

   a. rhythmic patterns
   b. melodic beauty
   c. polychords
   d. both a. and c.

8. The musical dynamics range from:

   a. ff to ppp
   b. mp to mf
   c. p to mp
   d. f to ff

9. The general effect of the excerpt is:

   a. relaxation
   b. tension
   c. primitive
   d. both b. and c.

10. This excerpt is from which section of the ballet?

   a. opening
   b. first part
   c. second part
   d. third part

Chapter 20. Expressionism: Atonal Music

Summary

Expression in art developed in Vienna during the early decades of the twentieth century. It focused on the "inner" world. In music, Schoenberg led this movement along with his colleagues Webern and Berg.

Schoenberg also created a new musical language that is characterized by melodies and harmonies carefully constructed to avoid creating tonal centers.

This is called atonality and once again his colleagues followed his lead.

By 1923, Schoenberg had formulated a theoretical system for composing atonal music - this system is known as serial, twelve-tone, or dodecaphonic composition. Central to his system are the rules that define the creation of a row and its subsequent manipulation.

Study Questions

1. Expressionism is centered on:

    a. the inner world
    b. the music of Debussy
    c. the art world in Paris
    d. the acceptance of Impressionism

2. Since the 1600's, what had been used, bent, and stretched by composers?

    a. Classical ideals
    b. the symphony orchestra
    c. the major-minor system of tonality
    d. the music of J. S. Bach

3. Which composer listed below was also the teacher of two other composers in this same list?

    a. Webern
    b. Berg
    c. Stravinsky
    d. Schoenberg

4. Which expressionistic opera depicts the torment and anxiety of the common man?

   a. Lulu
   b. Wozzeck
   c. Lyric Suite
   d. Das Augenlicht

5. At the core of the twelve-tone system is:

   a. a strict set of rules
   b. a tone row
   c. the chromatic scale
   d. all of the above

6. Which composer did not use the twelve-tone system?

   a. Debussy
   b. Webern
   c. Berg
   d. Schoenberg

7. Although the rows are primarily melodic, they can also provide a source for:

   a. rhythm
   b. instruments
   c. harmony
   d. dynamics

8. A composer can manipulate a row by:

   a. retrograde
   b. inversion
   c. retrograde inversion
   d. all of the above

Listening Self-Test

Schoenberg, Suite for Piano. C.D. No. 4, track 2.

9. The primary row is stated:

   a. at the beginning
   b. several times in succession
   c. after the introduction
   d. all of the above

10. The row is stated in the:

    a. middle register of the piano
    b. upper register of the piano
    c. in the lowest register of the piano
    d. several times in succession

11. How many notes of the row are stated before Schoenberg begins to imitate it using a different register?

    a. two
    b. three
    c. four
    d. the entire twelve tones

12. The form of this movement is:

    a. modified sonata
    b. theme and variations
    c. free
    d. retrograde

Chapter 21. Neoclassicism: Mainstream Music

Summary

Taking inspiration from the music of the Baroque and Classical periods, Stravinsky adapted these forms, idioms, and sounds to his own personal tastes. While in exile in Switzerland, he turned to smaller forces and created the style we now call Neoclassicism.

Neoclassicism is an approach to musical composition - it is not really a style period. With his piece the Octet (1922), his shift to Neoclassicism was complete. And with the exception of a brief encounter with atonal music, Stravinsky composed Neoclassical music for the rest of his life.

Another Russian composer who pursued the course of Neoclassicism was Sergei Prokofiev. His Symphony No. 1 is subtitled "Classical Symphony" because it follows the standard four-movement symphony of the late eighteenth-century in style and proportion.

Shostakovich, an accomplished pianist, also embraced the ideals of Neoclassicism. To continue composing, Shostakovich often had to sign apologies to the public because his music did not serve the needs of the Stalin regime.

Viewed broadly, Neoclassicism was an attempt to move back to the mainstream of music.

Other late nineteenth and early twentieth century European composers include:

United Kingdom - Elgar, Vaughan Williams, Holst, Walton, Britten and Grainger. While England had relatively few prominent native composers until the twentieth century, since then a number of prominent composers has emerged.

In France - Satie, Honegger, Milhaud, and Poulenc.
The music of Satie influenced the other three composers. He was opposed to impressionism and his music is often anti-sentimental and strident.

In Germany - Hindemith, Weill, and Orff.
Hindemith created a collection of works with a broad appeal which he called Gebrauchsmusik or "useful music." Hindemith also collaborated with Weill.

In Italy - Respighi.
Respighi wrote in both Neoclassical and impressionistic styles.

In Central Europe - Bartók.
Bartók collected, edited, and captured the essence Hungarian of folk music in his own music.

Hebrew - Bloch.
Ernest Bloch was an international musician influenced by his Jewish heritage.

Latin America - Villa-Lobos and Chavez.
The music of Villa-Lobos incorporates Brazilian folk materials while Chavez incorporates North American Indian folk tunes into his music.

Study Questions

1. The Neoclassic style is:

   a. a style
   b. a style period
   c. an approach to composition
   d. the extension of Romanticism

2. Stravinsky borrowed ideas from which style periods?

   a. the Baroque
   b. the Classical
   c. the Medieval
   d. all of the above

3. Which composer reached the same conclusion about Neoclassicism when Stravinsky did?

   a. Shostakovich
   b. Prokofiev
   c. Rachmaninoff
   d. Scriabin

4. The subtitle for Prokofiev's Symphony No. 1 is the:

   a. "Neoclassical"
   b. "Jupiter"
   c. "Titan"
   d. "Classical"

5. Prokofiev's Symphony No. 1 is closest in style to which composer?

a. Mozart
b. Haydn
c. Beethoven
d. Brahms

6. Which two composers had the most in common?

a. Stravinsky and Scriabin
b. Debussy and Prokofiev
c. Shostakovich and Prokofiev
d. Stravinsky and Shostakovich

7. In the general sense, Neoclassicism can be seen as:

a. a logical extension of Romanticism
b. a reaction to Impressionism
c. an attempt to move back to the mainstream of music
d. the beginnings of yet another style period

8. Which region of the world produced the composers Elgar, Walton, and Percy Grainger?

a. Spain
b. United Kingdom
c. Ecuador
d. Yugoslavia

Fill in the Blank

9. Paul Hindemith stands out as ____________ (country) most important twentieth century composer.

10. The collection of thirteenth century songs and poems that Carl Orff based a piece of music on was the ____________ ____________ .

11. Three Penny Opera (1928) was written by Kurt ____________ .

12. Bartók collected and edited ____________ folk music.

13. Elgar is perhaps best known for his ________ and ____________ marches.

14 A prolific English composer of the mid-twentieth century was Benjamin ______________ .

15. Honegger, Poulenc, and Milhaud were all influenced by the French composer Eric ________ .

Listening Self-Test

Prokofiev, Symphony No. 1, C.D. No. 4, track 2.

First Movement

16. The overall form of this movement is:

    a. Classical in design
    b. in a sonata form
    c. similar to Haydn's
    d. all of the above

17. The first theme is very:

    a. rhythmic
    b. flowing
    c. slow
    d. romantic

18. Which instruments dominate the orchestration?

    a. the strings
    b. the woodwinds
    c. the brass
    d. the percussion

19. The tempo of this movement is:

    a. steady and consistent
    b. slow
    c. allegro
    d. both a. and c.

20. The piece is neoclassic because:

    a. it is a new style
    b. it has elements of prior style periods
    c. it was written during the Classical period
    d. none of the above

Chapter 22. Experimental and Technological Music

Summary

During the first half of the twentieth century, the momentum of progress created radical changes in music. Traditionalism was the past while the future was experimentalism. Major trends during this time include: musique concrète, electronic music, computer music, mixed media music, aleatoric and chance music.

French composers used the term musique concrète to refer to everyday sounds that were recorded and then manipulated on tape recorders. Edgar Varèse was one composer who saw the possibilities in this process.

Electronic music refers to sounds produced on electronic oscillators and then recorded and stored. At first, this designation was used to distinguish man-made sounds from natural sounds (musique concrète). The synthesizer has revolutionized this process.

Computer and mixed media - invented in 1942, the computer may prove to be the most important invention in the world. MIDI is the language that allows computers and synthesizers to communicate. Sampling is the storage of sounds on computer disc.

Aleatoric music leaves the control of many aspects of musical performance in the hands of the performer. Chance music is similar to aleatoric music but is less precise in its instructions. Another important structural element is silence - as seen in the piece 4' 33" by John Cage. Other experimental composers include Boulez, Stockhausen, Penderecki, Glass, and Reich.

Study Questions

1. Musique concrète refers to:

    a. an experimental form of musical composition
    b. the recording and manipulation of man-made sounds
    c. the recording and manipulation of natural sounds
    d. both a. and b.

2. Techniques of musique concrète include:

    a. splicing and cutting
    b. overdubbing
    c. changing the speed
    d. all of the above

3. Electronic music refers to:

   a. sounds produced on electronic oscillators
   b. the recording and manipulation of man-made sounds
   c. the recording and manipulation of natural sounds
   d. both a. and b.

4. Early synthesizers were criticized for producing music that was:

   a. just real instruments
   b. too precise
   c. too synthetic
   d. both b. and c.

5. Lesemann's Metakinetic Invention, Version 2, is an example of:

   a. the diversity of electronic sounds
   b. the versatility of electronic music
   c. an advanced form of twelve-tone composition
   d. both a. and b.

6. MIDI is :

   a. musical instrument digital interface
   b. a language by which computers and synthesizers "talk"
   c. both a. and b.
   d. none of the above

7. Compared to aleatoric music, chance music is:

   a. more precise in its notation
   b. less precise in its notation
   c. essentially the same in notation and performance
   d. a non-improvisatory form of music

8. In essence, chance music is similar to:

   a. jazz
   b. the music of Schoenberg
   c. expressionism
   d. improvisational theater

9. Another composer who worked with musique concrète was:

   a. Boulez
   b. Penderecki
   c. Stockhausen
   d. Stravinsky

10. Philip Glass and Steve Reich are often referred to as composers of:

   a. expressionism
   b. folk music
   c. computer music
   d. minimalism

Listening Self-Test

Lesemann, <u>Metakinetic Invention</u>, Version 2. C.D. No. 4, track 4.

11. This excerpt displays:

   a. the versatility of electronic music
   b. neoclassical formal designs
   c. many elements of Romanticism
   d. elements of jazz improvisation

12. All of the techniques used on this piece:

   a. were performed on real instruments
   b. were performed on an electronic instrument
   c. are from combinations of real and electronic instruments
   d. none of the above

13. Which of the following are constantly changing?

   a. pitch
   b. timbre
   c. loudness
   d. all of the above

Chapter 23. Music in the United States

Summary

The influx of artists from Europe helped elevate the standards of American orchestras. America also became a refuge for some of the world's greatest composers and musicians.

Except for brief periods of federal funding, the arts in America have had to rely on ticket sales, private patrons, and corporate sponsorship.

Charles Ives was the first outstanding, distinctly American composer. In essence, Ives was an American nationalist. He attended Yale University and was very successful as an insurance salesman. He was a musical experimenter predating Stravinsky in his use of polychord, polymeter, etc. Ives enjoyed combining different ensembles in different keys. In his patriotic works he tried to convey the American spirit he acquired during his New England childhood. His piece, "Putnam's Camp," from the Three Places in New England is an example of this.

Jazz is an American art form. Several ingredients came together to produce this distinctive style of American music including African singing, European church music, the blues, and African-American Church music.

Call and response, riffs, and ostinatos are all vocal techniques that were combined with African rhythms, syncopations, and polyrhythms to create a distinct sound. All that was needed was the addition of European harmony and jazz had its origins.

Military bands influenced the beginnings of instrumental jazz, as did the funeral procession, the cakewalk, and ragtime. Scott Joplin was known as the king of ragtime.

Bridging the gap between classical and jazz was George Gershwin. His last important musical contribution, and perhaps his greatest, is his opera Porgy and Bess, written in 1935. The opera is based on a novel, Porgy, and Gershwin envisioned it as the basis for a distinctly American folk opera. The setting is Catfish Row, an African-American community in South Carolina.

Another important American composer is Aaron Copland. His music is very eclectic as can be seen in his old west ballet Rodeo. Important for his contributions as a composer and a conductor is Leonard Bernstein. His musical output includes West Side Story, Mass, and the comic operetta Candide.

Other American composers include Menotti (opera composer), Schuman, Piston, Sessions, Barber, and Hanson.

Study Questions

1. Despite popular appeal, the arts in the U. S. have always faced:

   a. a lack of ticket sales
   b. a dwindling audience
   c. a lack of significant financial support from the government
   d. a lack of exposure

2. Many of the experimental techniques of Charles Ives actually predate:

   a. those of Wagner
   b. those of Stravinsky
   c. the development of the computer
   d. the development of twelve-tone music

3. Ives wrote more music about which holiday?

   a. Fourth of July
   b. Easter
   c. Christmas
   d. Columbus Day

4. One of his favorite devices was to use:

   a. texts from European art songs
   b. accompaniments in contrasting keys
   c. extensive development sections
   d. Schoenberg's atonality

5. Why was Ives not concerned whether or not anyone liked his music?

   a. He was only experimenting.
   b. He had no musical training.
   c. He did not rely on composing for his livelihood.
   d. He only wrote it for himself anyway.

6. The juxtaposition of seemingly unrelated tunes and situations is called:

   a. polytonality
   b. polymedia
   c. polymeter
   d. polychords

7. The breeding ground for jazz was:

   a. Chicago
   b. New York
   c. Philadelphia
   d. New Orleans

8. Instrumental jazz was affected by:

   a. European church music
   b. African singing
   c. the Blues
   d. African rhythms

9. Call and Response is:

   a. an element of vocal jazz
   b. an early form of African vocal music
   c. still an integral part of African-American church services
   d. all of the above

10. A "riff" is most similar to a(n):

   a. fugue
   b. development section
   c. ostinato
   d. jagged melody

11. The use of syncopation is a:

   a. rhythmic device
   b. melodic device
   c. tone color
   d. meter

12. The overlay of several conflicting rhythms is called:

   a. polymeter
   b. polytempo
   c. polyrhythm
   d. none of the above

13. The blues scale conveys a feeling of:

   a. singing
   b. sadness
   c. working
   d. anger

14. Military bands could be found at:

    a. important occasions
    b. parades
    c. funerals
    d. all of the above

15. The cakewalk is a:

    a. high-kicking dance
    b. dance competition for a cake
    c. dance that originated on Southern plantations
    d. all of the above

16. Around the turn of the century the cakewalk was renamed:

    a. syncopation
    b. swing
    c. ragtime
    d. blues

17. The composers Piston, Sessions, and Barber:

    a. are American composers
    b. show Neoclassical influences in their music
    c. both a. and b.
    d. none of the above

Matching

18. The "King of Ragtime" was?
19. George Gershwin worked on Tin Pan Alley doing?
20. Gershwin incorporated elements of which style into his music?
21. The opera Porgy and Bess was based on this.
22. Copland received a series of these commissions.
23. In the "Hoedown" from Rodeo, Copland used what kind of music in order to create an authentic spirit and sound?
24. The composer of the musical West Side Story is?
25. The composer Menotti is best known for what?

Allan Tudzin
Scott Joplin
operetta
L. Bernstein
ballets
song plugger
novel
teacher
poetry
symphonies
rock and roll
painter
songs
jazz
Marsocci
country fiddle
L. Stuart
operas

Listening Self-Test

Ives, "Memories." C.D. No. 4, track 6.

26. What type of piece is this?

    a. an aria
    b. a song
    c. lieder
    d. recitative

27. This piece shows what attributes of Ives?

    a. his wit
    b. his experimentation
    c. his affinity for jazz
    d. none of the above

28. The portrait is one of:

    a. a theatrical production
    b. excitement
    c. an opera house
    d. all of the above

Ives, "Putnam's Camp" from Three Places in New England. C.D. No. 4, track 6.

29. The opening to "Putnam's Camp" is played by the:

    a. full orchestra
    b. chamber group
    c. only the strings
    d. only the woodwinds

30. The tempo at the beginning is:

    a. slow
    b. moderate
    c. fast
    d. very slow

31. The opening style is that of a:

    a. funeral dirge
    b. march
    c. quick step
    d. both b. and c.

32. The main march tune at the beginning is:

a. in a duple meter
b. in a triple meter
c. mainly monophonic
d. played by the woodwinds and brass

Gershwin, "Bess, You Is My Woman Now," from Porgy and Bess. C. D. No. 4, track 8.

33. Porgy is sung by a:

a. bass
b. tenor
c. baritone
d. countertenor

34. Bess is sung by a(n):

a. alto
b. mezzo-soprano
c. soprano
d. tenor

35. The mood of the piece is generally:

a. fast
b. in a state of constant flux
c. relaxed
d. very slow and ponderous

36. Gershwin moves from the beginning of the song to the end by:

a. imitating
b. repeating sections
c. changing keys
d. none of the above

Copland, "Hoedown" from Rodeo. C.D. No. 4, track 7.

37. In the very beginning, the first tune is a:

a. fiddle tune
b. blues progression
c. ragtime piece
d. blues scale

38. The meter of the piece is:

a. duple
b. triple
c. mixed
d. polymeter

39. What happens in the second rhythmic interlude?

a. the tempos speeds up
b. there is a crescendo
c. there is a use of rubato
d. both a. and b.

Chapter 24. American Popular Music

Summary

It is often very difficult to draw a dividing line between popular and classical music. Today, the main distinction between the two is that popular music is created to be commercially successful. Often, because of its appeal, its popularity is short-lived. Classical music, however, sustains itself from generation to generation by appealing to a more selective audience.

Stephen Foster is an example of a composer who wrote hundreds of songs in the nineteenth century. When Irving Berlin wrote the popular song "Alexander's Ragtime Band" in 1911, jazz crossed over into popular music. Until this time, jazz had been the sole province of black musicians. By 1916, jazz was sweeping across the nation.

Tin Pan Alley was a commercial hub of American popular music. In order to hear the latest tunes of the day, one had to go either to the theater or to a department store where song pluggers would play the music and try to sell you the sheet music.

With the mass production of phonograph records, radio broadcasts, and the dawn of the "talkie" movie, a new market for popular music was being created.

In the 1930's and 1940's the swing era was in full force. Many of the big bands featured a male and female vocalist. To boost the morale of the allied troops during World War II, many big band's performances were broadcast throughout the war zones.

In order to increase production during World War II, factories introduced music. As a result of various studies, environmental music emerged. In theory, you don't have to listen to the music - it is designed to surround you and help shape your mood.

Due to a variety of economic reasons, after World War II the costly big band era ended as small groups became fashionable. The jukebox became an economical replacement for live music. The Grand Ole Opry and other country music broadcasts made Nashville, Tennessee, a significant center for country music.

Rhythm and blues was a transitional style between swing and rock. With the organization of Motown Records, R & B became even stronger in the 1960's. Rock and roll was originally a musical potpourri of jazz, blues, rhythm and blues, folk, and country.

Important contributors to early rock and roll include Bill Haley and the Comets, Elvis Presley, the Beatles, the Byrds, and the Rolling Stones.

Folk-rock music played an important part at the 1969 Woodstock Festival. The festival promoted such causes as civil rights and the end of the Vietnam War. Also in the late 1960's jazz-rock and the use of electronic instruments came into vogue. Some of the characteristics of live rock performances include: an amplified bass, ostinato rhythms, modal harmonies, electronic synthesizers, costumes, and light shows.

Study Questions

1. The main distinction between popular and classical music is:

   a. a matter of taste
   b. popular music is commercially designed
   c. classical music is more selective in its appeal
   d. both b. and c.

2. Which of the following is not an early American popular music style?

   a. jazz-rock
   b. work songs
   c. spirituals
   d. cowboy songs

3. The composer of "Oh, Susanna!" and "Camptown Races" is:

   a. Scott Joplin
   b. Stephen Foster
   c. James DiCoco
   d. Irving Berlin

4. The first jazz song to become commercially successful was:

   a. "Oh, Susanna!"
   b. "Maple Leaf Rag"
   c. "Rhapsody in Blue"
   d. "Alexander's Ragtime Band"

5. Tin Pan Alley got its name from:

   a. a street sign
   b. the section of town
   c. the piano sounds of song pluggers
   d. a prominent businessman

6. Which of the following did not help to popularize early music in America?

   a. Edison's wind-up phonograph
   b. Marconi's crystal radio
   c. home radio sets
   d. both a. and b.

7. From which decade did the first "talkie" come?

   a. the 1920's
   b. the 1930's
   c. the 1940's
   d. the 1950's

8. The big bands played swing music for:

   a. radio commercials
   b. listening and dancing
   c. improvisation
   d. television

9. The term "crooner" refers to a(n):

   a. lead trumpet player
   b. mute for a brass instrument
   c. vocalist
   d. type of dance

10. Which big band leader joined the Army Air Force during World War II?

    a. Glenn Miller
    b. Tommy Dorsey
    c. Jimmy Dorsey
    d. Duke Ellington

11. Music that is designed to shape your mood is called:

    a. mood music
    b. relaxation music
    c. environmental music
    d. stylized music

12. After World War II:

    a. the big band era flourished
    b. jazz music died out
    c. small combos came into style
    d. none of the above

13. Which of the following did not occur after World War II?

    a. the jukebox
    b. popularization of county music
    c. popularization of rhythm and blues
    d. continuation of the swing band era

14. Melody and text are subordinate to:

    a. the rhythms of rock
    b. the syncopations of jazz
    c. the harmonies of folk music
    d. the electric guitar

15. Many of the Beatles' songs are:

    a. about the absurdity of war
    b. a protest of the Establishment
    c. considered standards today
    d. all of the above

16. Jazz-rock incorporates:

    a. elements of rhythm and blues
    b. trumpets, trombones, and electronic instruments
    c. Classical music forms
    d. folk-rock elements

Chapter 25. American Musical Theater

Summary

Predecessors of the musical include the ballad opera, comic opera, and the pasticcio. The ballad opera had spoken dialogue between songs instead of recitative. It also had popular tunes and folk songs set to original lyrics.

The comic opera incorporated the English emphasis of comedy over romance while the pasticcio was a cross between ballad opera and comic opera. The most popular eighteenth century pasticcio was John Gay's The Beggar's Opera of 1728.

The majority of American musicals fall into several broad categories: musical comedy, musical play, modern operetta, popular opera, and play with music.

The musical comedy is usually a good story with a comical theme. For example, Annie, Get Your Gun and Oklahoma.

In a musical play the drama predominates while the music and lyrics support the substance of the plot (Les Misérables), while in a play with music the story must stand alone (My Fair Lady).

A modern operetta blends sentimentality of the past with present-day values while popular opera embraces the old conventions of opera: everything is set to music.

Minstrel shows of the nineteenth century were the first all-American musical theater productions. "Dixie" was the best-known minstrel song of its day.

Vaudeville's roots go back to a fifteenth century village known as Val-de-Vire in Normandy, France. The American stage version was a succession of unrelated specialty acts. It could include such diverse elements as singers, jugglers, fire-eaters, Swiss bell ringers, and anything that was sensational and startling. Some of America's most popular songs emerged from vaudeville including "In the Good Old Summertime" and "My Wild Irish Rose."

Burlesque was raucous and bawdy. Starting in the late 1860's, touring companies played to audiences of men eager for grown- up entertainment. After World War I burlesque declined into a vulgar sexuality.

The extravaganza/spectacular could be seen at New York's Hippodrome Theater which could hold 5,200 paying customers and could fit over six hundred performers on the stage. Events held there included sensational water ballets, baseball games and cavalry charges.The American version of the revue was an energetic, nonbook show built around star performers. Featured were musical selections, comedy acts, dramatic sketches, and specialty routines.

On Broadway, the longest-running annual revue was the Ziegfeld Follies. From 1907 to 1931 twenty-five editions were held. Florenz Ziegfeld commissioned over 500 songs from composers like Jerome Kern, Victor Herbert, and Irving Berlin.

Operetta, originating in Germany and the Austro-Hungarian Empire, incorporated every aspect of late-nineteenth-century romanticism within a trivial plot. It was refined and introduced to the American audiences shortly after the turn of the twentieth century by Victor Herbert, Sigmund Romberg, and Rudolf Friml. The Great Depression affected operetta as it had the extravaganza/spectacular.

Some of the roots of modern American musical comedy can be found in the works of George M. Cohan. His "plays with music" were full of songs created for singing actors and not operetta singers. While the first black musical opened in 1903, a number of African-Americans have enriched the world of musical theater including Will Marion Cook and Paul Lawrence Dunbar.

Both Irving Berlin and Jerome Kern contributed to the legacy of musical theater. Kern's Show Boat of 1927 was a milestone in that it demonstrated that dramatic literature could merge with romantic song with the end result being successful musical theater. After Kern left Broadway, his lyricist, Oscar Hammerstein II, teamed up with Richard Rodgers to continue the tradition Kern had begun. Their musical plays include South Pacific, Carousel, The King and I, and The Sound of Music.

George and Ira Gershwin were a remarkable collaboration in musical theater, while Cole Porter brought elements of extraordinary style and sophistication to the stage.

Learning from the genius of Hammerstein, Stephen Sondheim's scores give the actor something to act - a theatrical moment. He made his Broadway debut as a lyricist for West Side Story in 1957 and has won several Tony Awards for his work.

Leonard Bernstein also wrote several major works for the American musical stage including West Side Story and Wonderful Town. Set in one of New York City's ethnically mixed neighborhoods, West Side Story was inspired by Shakespeare's Romeo and Juliet.

Study Questions

1. The term "book" refers to:

   a. all of the dramatic action in a musical
   b. the story of the musical
   c. the lyrics of the the songs
   d. the program of the performance

2. The roots of the musical are ballad opera, comic opera, and the:

   a. minstrel
   b. revue
   c. pasticcio
   d. opera bouffe

3. Which of the following is not a category of American musicals?

   a. musical comedy
   b. popular opera
   c. play with music
   d. spectacle/extravaganza

4. Gershwin's Porgy and Bess is a:

   a. modern operetta
   b. popular opera
   c. play with music
   d. minstrel

5. The most important African-American writer who joined the minstrel troupes after World War I was:

   a. James A. Bland
   b. Dan Emmett
   c. Tony Pastor
   d. Stephen Foster

6. Vaudeville had its roots in:

   a. the South
   b. New England
   c. France
   d. London

7. "In the Good Old Summertime" and "My Wild Irish Rose" are both:

   a. opera numbers
   b. swing band numbers
   c. popular songs from vaudeville
   d. titles of musical comedies

8. Burlesque is different from vaudeville because of the nature of its:

   a. intended audience
   b. subject matter
   c. moral character
   d. all of the above

9. The Great Depression had a disastrous effect on the:

   a. play with music
   b. minstrels
   c. extravaganza/spectacle
   d. popular plays

10. The original revue was:

   a. a satire of Parisian high life
   b. a French variety show
   c. developed in the south
   d. both a. and b.

11. The revue reached its height:

   a. in the Southern states only
   b. in England and North America between the wars
   c. in France where it had originated
   d. none of the above

12. Eddie Cantor, Will Rogers, and W.C. Fields were all stars "made" by:

   a. George Gershwin
   b. Bruce Tellier
   c. Jerome Kern
   d. Florenz Ziegfeld

13. A trivial plot combined with appealing music and dance is a(n):

   a. ballet
   b. operetta
   c. musical
   d. stage show

14. One of the greatest hits of Victor Herbert was his:

    a. Three Musketeers
    b. Porgy and Bess
    c. Babes in Toyland
    d. Student Prince

15. George M. Cohan's Little Johnny Jones contained the hit song:

    a. "Oh, Susanna!"
    b. "Yankee Doodle Dandy"
    c. "Summertime"
    d. "Lazy River"

16. The first black musical to open at a whites-only Broadway theater:

    a. was first performed in 1903
    b. was entitled In Dahomey
    c. was written by Will Cook and Paul Dunbar
    d. all of the above

17. Jerome Kern insisted upon:

    a. more money for his music
    b. the importance of the story
    c. a partnership between the story and the music
    d. more dramatic action to accompany his music

18. Joe, the vocalist in the song "Ol' Man River," earns a living by:

    a. driving a tugboat
    b. selling supplies
    c. loading bales of cotton
    d. driving a truck

Fill in the Blank

19. George Gershwin wrote the music while his brother, Ira, was his ________________ .

20. After Kern left Broadway, his lyricist Hammerstein II teamed up with Richard ______________ .

21. The songs of Sondheim show an understanding of dramatic ________________ .

22. West Side Story was inspired by Shakespeare's ______________ and ______________ .

Listening Self-Test

Kern, "Ol' Man River" from <u>Showboat</u>. C.D. No 4, track 10.

23. The voice that is singing the lead is:

    a. a tenor
    b. light and airy
    c. a bass
    d. an alto

24. The meter of the piece is:

    a. duple
    b. triple
    c. mixed
    d. polymeter

25. The vocalist frequently uses:

    a. crescendo
    b. timbre
    c. rubato
    d. both a. and c.

Rodgers & Hammerstein, "Opening Chorus," <u>Oklahoma</u>. C.D. no. 4, track 11.

26. The mood at the opening is one of:

    a. sadness
    b. melancholy
    c. jubilant
    d. patriotism

27. The tempo is:

    a. duple
    b. triple
    c. allegro
    d. grave

28. Who does most of the singing?

    a. the soloist
    b. the chorus
    c. the chorus and soloist
    d. none of the above

Sondheim, "Send in the Clowns" from A Little Night Music. C.D. No. 4, track 13.

29. The unusual instrument you hear is a(n):

   a. trumpet
   b. piccolo
   c. English horn
   d. oboe

30. What is the overall mood of the work?

   a. happy
   b. melancholy
   c. horror
   d. romance

31. The vocalist uses what technique to create a feeling of expression?

   a. con sordino
   b. poco a poco
   c. rubato
   d. ostinato

32. The tempo of the song is:

   a. fairly slow
   b. steady throughout
   c. allegro
   d. lively and quick

Bernstein, "Tonight" from West Side Story, C.D. No. 4, track 12.

33. This piece begins with a(n):

   a. overture
   b. introduction
   c. modulation
   d. vocalist

34. The first melody of this piece is:

   a. rhythmic
   b. lyric
   c. melodic
   d. smooth

35. The second melody, in contrast to the first, is much more:

a. lyric
b. harmonic
c. rhythmic
d. atonal

36. Overall, the tempo of the piece is:

a. grave
b. ritardando
c. allegro
d. crescendo

Wilson, "76 Trombones" from The Music Man, C.D. No. 4, track 14.

37. What follows the 76 trombones?

a. trumpets
b. clarinets
c. cornets
d. tubas

38. Overall, the tempo of the piece is:

a. vivace
b. sostenuto
c. march-like
d. crescendo

39. The meter of this piece is:

a. duple
b. triple
c. allegro
d. grave

Bock, "Sunrise, Sunset" from Fiddler on the Roof. C.D. No. 4, track 15.

40. This piece begins with a(n):

a. soloist
b. introduction
c. ostinato
d. overture

41. The meter of the piece is:

a. duple
b. triple
c. allegro
d. grave

42. This song is actually a(n):

a. operetta
b. duet
c. recitative
d. aria

Chapter 26. Music for Films

Summary

Music and movies have a unique relationship. Music is an essential ingredient to the overall entertainment, action, and emotion of the scene.

It began in 1908 when composer Camille Saint-Saëns composed a film score for the movie The Assassination of the Duke of Guise. Within five years, publishers had catalogued their music for theater orchestras, pianists, or organists to play according to the specific needs of the movie scenes.

Max Winkler made up music cue sheets for all of the Universal Film Company movies and eventually went to work full time in film music. Any work not under copyright was fair game, but often significant changes were made to pieces in order to fit the mood of the scene.

While the score to D.W. Griffith's The Birth of a Nation established standards for orchestration and cuing, the German composer Edmund Meisel devised a distinctive system for analyzing film montages to determine the timing of the music needed. With the advent of sound films in 1927 the music track displaced live performances. And during the 1930's, many composers associated with concert music wrote original scores for films.

It was Walt Disney who added a new element to the partnership of music and film in his classic Fantasia. His advancement was the development of a machine that synchronized the sound with the animation.

The composer Aaron Copland has said that the atmosphere of a movie is "color" and that "Music creates a psychological element better than dialogue can."

Just as Wagner used the principle of leitmotif, so does the composer John Williams use a musical idea to represent the important character(s) in a movie.

Study Questions

1. The relationship of music to film is:

    a. antagonistic
    b. a unique relationship
    c. unsettling
    d. emotional

2. Music gives what to the film medium?

   a. heightened drama
   b. suspense
   c. romance
   d. life to the film

3. In 1908, the first composer to write a film score was:

   a. Stravinsky
   b. Schoenberg
   c. Ives
   d. Saint-Saëns

4. Max Winkler's profession before he entered the film music business was that of a:

   a. composer
   b. musician
   c. cataloguer
   d. pianist

5. Many works by the great masters were:

   a. used in films
   b. not protected by copyright
   c. changed to suit the need of the movie
   d. all of the above

6. The "master" of the silent film score was:

   a. Saint-Saëns
   b. Meisel
   c. Nevsky
   d. Potemkin

7. Which composer wrote a new score as a synchronized sound track for the movie Napoleon?

   a. John Williams
   b. Steve Adams
   c. Bruce Broughton
   d. Carmine Coppola

8. What invention displaced the need for live performances with silent movies?

   a. the movie cue
   b. the tape recorder
   c. the music track
   d. none of the above

9. Which movie featured synchronized sound with animation?

   a. Superman
   b. Fantasia
   c. The Street Singer
   d. Rio Rita

10. According to Aaron Copland, the atmosphere of time and place in a movie is called:

    a. neutral background
    b. intensifier
    c. color
    d. aesthetics

11. In order to represent various characters, composers often use:

    a. a leitmotif
    b. the process of overdubbing
    c. natural and synthetic sounds
    d. all of the above

12. The concept of Ubermensch is:

    a. the German for superman
    b. a doctrine promoted by Nietzsche
    c. a nineteenth-century German subject
    d. all of the above

13. The movie Silverado is set in the:

    a. Canadian Yukon
    b. Australian Outback
    c. New England
    d. American West

Listening Self-Test

Williams, "Love Theme" from <u>Superman</u>. C.D. No. 4, track 16.

14. The very beginning uses a rhythmic device know as a(n):

    a. ostinato
    b. chaccone
    c. fugue
    d. stretto

15. Which family of instruments dominates the melody?

    a. woodwinds
    b. keyboards
    c. brass
    d. percussion

16. The meter of the piece is:

    a. duple
    b. triple
    c. mixed
    d. unstable

Broughton, "End Credits" from <u>Silverado</u>. C.D. No. 4, track 17.

17. The main theme is first introduced by which instruments?

    a. clarinets
    b. horns
    c. trombones
    d. strings

18. Which instrument imitates the instrument from question #1?

    a. flute
    b. tuba
    c. trumpet
    d. oboe

19. The tempo at the very beginning is:

    a. slow
    b. fast
    c. lively
    d. ritard

20. Once the main theme is introduced, Broughton changes the:

   a. meter
   b. sequence
   c. tempo
   d. all of the above

Chapter 27. Contributions of World Cultures

Summary

While the focus of this book has been on music encountered in North American and European concert halls, there is a wealth of folk and ethnic music around us. The field of ethnomusicology deals with the music of world cultures.

It was during the World Expositions that the major centers featured non-Western performing groups. Many composers were influenced by the musical experiences they encountered throughout their travels. At the Paris Exposition in 1889 musicians came to see and hear a large array of ethnic music groups perform.

Western composers often incorporate non-Western instruments like the xylophone (Africa), cymbals (Turkey), conga drum (South America), and the tam tam (Chinese gong).

Music south of the Sahara encompasses over 50 countries. Hardly a tribal or religious activity of African daily life takes place without music. African music is passed orally from generation to generation. Musical notation is very rare.
In addition to the contributions to the percussion family, African musicians use a variety of flutelike instruments, animal horns, and stringed instruments.

At the core of their music is rhythm, especially the device known as polyrhythm. Constantly changing rhythms and metrical groupings are important characteristics of this music. While there is a use of ostinato, many performers are free to improvise. As for their vocal music, it is composed of a variety of ostinato sounds.

The pentatonic scale is predominant in Africa, but there are microtones present in the music as well. Microtones fall in between the tones of Western music. One of the most important vocal techniques is the call and response that we discussed in the chapter on jazz.

Transplanted African musical developments include calypso music (Trinidad), the mambo and rumba (Cuba), the bossa nova and conga (Brazil), and reggae (Jamaica).

British, Islamic and Asian conquerors of India have shaped their music. The melodies of Indian music, for example, are organized into ragas and have similar counterparts in Iran and Islamic Middle Eastern music.

Cine music (film music), which is very popular in India, is a blend of East and West in that the Asian based scales can be heard over Latin-American rhythms. The punji, a form of gourd and reed bagpipe, can often be found in the hands of snake charmers.

The music of India is separated into two closely related traditions, North and South, which each style using a slightly different set of instruments. Contemporary groups like the Beatles and Paul Horn have recorded using Indian instruments (sitar) and musical techniques (ragas).

Japanese music is traceable to the third century B.C. while the gagaku court orchestra originated in the fifth century A.D. These gagaku orchestras can still be heard today. There is an abundance of solo and chamber music available for Japan's most popular instruments such as the koto, kokyu, and the shakuhachi flute.

At the heart of the Japanese music is the pentatonic (five note) scale. The popular "Sakura" or "Cherry Blossom" song uses this scale.

Much of the theater of Japan relies on musical accompaniment. The Kabuki theater and Nogaku musical plays are two examples. Because of the diverse Japanese cultural history, many of the Japanese musicians have studied Western music and the music of Mozart and Beethoven are as much the favorites in Japan as they are in Europe.

Study Questions

1. The music of world cultures would include music from:

   a. Africa
   b. India
   c. Japan
   d. all of the above

2. Ethnomusicology is the study of:

   a. European music
   b. Indian music
   c. world culture's music
   d. none of these

3. What event(s) helped to expose musicians to non-Western music?

   a. travel to distant lands
   b. World Expositions
   c. World War II
   d. both a. and b.

4. Which piece of music was influenced by the music of a non-Western culture?

   a. Romeo and Juliet
   b. Scheherazade
   c. The Pines of Rome
   d. 1812 Overture

5. Which of the following did not influence Debussy to use non-Western sounds in his music?

   a. Paris World Exposition
   b. Asian music ensembles
   c. exotic percussion instruments
   d. travel to Indonesia

6. Which non-Western instruments have been used by Western composers in their music?

   a. drums
   b. finger cymbals
   c. maracas
   d. all of the above

7. African music is:

   a. from an oral tradition
   b. notated
   c. based on harmony
   d. similar to Indian music

8. At the heart of African music is:

   a. melody
   b. polytonality
   c. rhythm
   d. harmony

9. Singers of African music need to use:

   a. a microphone
   b. ostinato chants
   c. notated music
   d. a drum beat

10. Call and Response is:

    a. an important part of early jazz
    b. of African origin
    c. a vocal technique
    d. all of the above

11. Reggae, calypso, and the conga are all:

    a. African chants
    b. African scales
    c. transplanted African influences
    d. the basis of the African call and response

12. The Suzuki Method is:

    a. method of teaching Western music to Japanese students
    b. a method book for the piano
    c. a method of teaching Japanese students in groups
    d. a form of music used by the Kabuki theater

13. Japanese musicians are:

    a. familiar with Western music
    b. deeply rooted in a purely written tradition
    c. able to trace their heritage back to the third century B.C.
    d. both a. and c.

Matching

14. The music of India has:

15. "Cine music" is:

16. A punji is a(n):

17. A pentatonic scale is a(n):

a non-oral tradition
reed bagpipe
two traditions
street theater
five note scale
Iida music
film music
sitar

ANSWERS

Chapter 1.

1. c
2. d
3. c
4. a
5. a
6. d

Chapter 2.

1. a
2. d
3. a
4. d
5. b
6. c
7. c

Chapter 3.

1. d
2. b
3. d
4. a
5. d
6. c
7. a
8. c
9. a
10. c
11. b
12. c
13. b
14. c

Chapter 4.

1. c
2. b
3. a
4. c
5. b
6. d
7. b
8. c
9. c
10. d
11. d
12. d
13. b
14. a
15. c
16. c
17. b
18. c
19. a
20. Stravinsky
21. organ
22. harpsichord
23. tenor
24. c
25. a
26. c
27. d
28. d
29. c

Chapter 5.

1. c
2. d
3. d
4. a
5. d
6. c
7. c

Chapter 6.

1. plainchant, plainsong
2. monophonic
3. Proper, Ordinary
4. troubadour, trouvere
5. organum
6. Latin
7. Gregory 1st
8. secular
9. Age of Faith
10. Judaic
11. a
12. c
13. c
14. c
15. a
16. c
17. b
18. a
19. b
20. c
21. polyphonic
22. Humanism
23. art and philosophy
24. chamber
25. Court
26. Italy
27. lute
28. 5
29. Rome
30. Leonardo da Vinci
31. c
32. c
33. c
34. a
35. a
36. a
37. a

Chapter 7.

1. c
2. d
3. d
4. d
5. b
6. d
7. b
8. a
9. c
10. d

Chapter 8.

1. a
2. d
3. b
4. d
5. c
6. a
7. b
8. d
9. d
10. c
11. d
12. a
13. a
14. a
15. 3 part
16. concertos
17. fugue
18. oratorio
19. coda
20. d
21. d
22. c
23. a
24. d
25. a
26. c
27. b
28. b
29. d
30. a
31. b
32. c
33. d
34. b
35. c
36. a
37. b
38. c
39. b
40. c
41. b
42. b
43. c

Chapter 9.

1. c
2. a
3. d
4. d
5. d
6. c
7. d
8. b
9. a
10. c

Chapter 10.

1. d
2. a
3. a
4. d
5. b
6. a
7. d
8. a
9. d
10. c
11. b
12. b
13. a
14. d
15. development
16. four
17. Mozart
18. folk theater
19. b
20. c
21. b
22. a
23. c
24. c
25. b
26. a
27. c
28. a
29. d
30. d
31. d
32. d
33. c
34. a
35. c
36. a
37. c
38. b
39. a
40. d
41. a
42. a
43. c
44. b
45. d
46. a
47. d
48. d

Chapter 11.

1. b
2. a
3. b
4. d
5. d
6. b
7. c
8. d
9. b
10. c
11. b
12. d
13. b
14. a
15. b
16. c
17. d
18. b
19. b
20. a
21. c
22. a
23. d
24. c
25. c
26. a
27. b
28. d
29. b
30. b

Chapter 12.

1. c
2. d
3. d
4. c
5. b
6. a
7. d
8. writers
9. program
10. emotional
11. fugue

Chapter 13.

1. d
2. b
3. c
4. b
5. d
6. b
7. a
8. d
9. d
10. d
11. c
12. a
13. a
14. c
15. d
16. c
17. d
18. piano
19. Robert Schumann
20. Clara Schumann
21. Chopin
22. Liszt
23. a
24. d
25. b
26. b
27. d
28. a
29. c
30. d
31. c
32. d
33. b
34. a
35. c
36. a
37. c
38. c
39. a
40. b

Chapter 14.

1. d
2. c
3. a
4. c
5. c
6. d
7. c
8. a
9. c
10. d
11. b
12. a
13. d
14. leitmotif
15. Meistersinger
16. operetta
17. verismo
18. d
19. b
20. c
21. d
22. c
23. b
24. d
25. d

Chapter 15.

1. c
2. a
3. b
4. c
5. a
6. c
7. b
8. b
9. d
10. "Titan"
11. Freud
12. horn
13. Brahms
14. Haydn
15. a
16. a
17. d
18. c
19. d
20. b
21. a
22. a
23. b
24. c
25. a
26. d

Chapter 16.

1. d
2. d
3. b
4. c
5. b
6. d
7. c
8. b
9. d
10. c
11. b
12. d
13. d
14 c
15. b
16. b
17. d
18. c
19. c
20. a
21. d
22. c
23. b

Chapter 17.

1. d
2. d
3. c
4. a
5. d
6. d
7. d
8. whole-tone
9. extend
10. Mallarme
11. Ravel
12. d
13. b
14. b
15. a

Chapter 18.

1. b
2. d
3. b
4. d
5. d
6. d
7. c
8. a
9. d
10. b

Chapter 19.

1. d
2. c
3. a
4. c
5. c
6. b
7. d
8. a
9. d
10. c

Chapter 20.

1. a
2. c
3. d
4. b
5. d
6. a
7. c
8. d
9. a
10. b
11. b
12. c

Chapter 21.

1. c
2. d
3. b
4. d
5. b
6. b
7. c
8. b
9. Germany's
10. <u>Carmina Burana</u>
11. Weill
12. Hungarian
13. <u>Pomp and Circumstance</u>
14. Britten
15. Satie
16. d
17. a
18. a
19. d
20. b

Chapter 22.

1. d
2. d
3. a
4. d
5. d
6. c
7. b
8. d
9. c
10. d
11. a
12. b
13. d

Chapter 23.

1. c
2. b
3. a
4. b
5. c
6. b
7. d
8. b
9. d
10. c
11. a
12. c
13. b
14. d
15. d
16. c
17. c
18. Scott Joplin
19. song plugger
20. jazz
21. novel
22. ballets
23. country fiddle
24. L. Bernstein
25. opera
26. b
27. b
28. d
29. a
30. c
31. c
32. a
33. a
34. c
35. c
36. b
37. a
38. a
39. c

Chapter 24.

1. b
2. a
3. b
4. d
5. c
6. d
7. a
8. b
9. c
10. a
11. c
12. c
13. d
14. a
15. d
16. b

Chapter 25.

1. b
2. c
3. d
4. b
5. a
6. c
7. c
8. d
9. c
10. d
11. b
12. d
13. b
14. c
15. b
16. d
17. c
18. c
19. lyricist
20. Rodgers
21. construction
22. Romeo and Juliet
23. a
24. a
25. d
26. c
27. c
28. c
29. b
30. b
31. c
32. a
33. b
34. a
35. a
36. c
37. c
38. c
39. a
40. b
41. a
42. b

Chapter 26.

1. b
2. d
3. d
4. c
5. d
6. b
7. d
8. c
9. b
10. c
11. a
12. d
13. d
14. a
15. c
16. a
17. b
18. c
19. a
20. c

Chapter 27.

1. d
2. c
3. d
4. b
5. d
6. d
7. a
8. c
9. b
10. d
11. c
12. c
13. d
14. two traditions
15. film music
16. reed bagpipe
17. five note scale

Appendix A

Checklists for Further Listening

Chapter 4 - The Interaction of Musical Elements

Orchestra and Orchestral Instruments:

- Beethoven, Symphony No. 5, First Movement
  Cassette Tape, Side C, Example 16
  Compact Disc No. 2, Track 3
- Brahms, Trio in E-Flat (horn, violin, piano)
  Cassette Tape, Side D, Example 23
  Compact Disc No. 2, Track 11
- Copland, Rodeo "Hoe Down"
  Cassette Tape, Side D, Example 29
  Compact Disc No. 4, Track 8
- Mahler, Symphony No. 1, First Movement
  Compact Disc No. 3, Track 3
- Mendelssohn, Violin Concerto, First Movement
  Compact Disc No. 2, Track 9
- Mozart, Symphony No. 40, four movements
  Cassette Tape, Side B, Example 14
  Compact Disc No. 1, Tracks 10 - 13
- Wagner, Die Meistersinger Overture
  Cassette Tape, Side C, Example 21
  Compact Disc No. 2, Track 10

Keyboards:

- Beethoven, Piano Sonata No. 8, Third Movement
  Cassette Tape, Side B, Example 11
  Compact Disc No. 2, Track 2
- Mozart, Piano Concerto No. 21, Third Movement
  Cassette Tape, Side B, Example 12
  Compact Disc No. 1, Track 14

Voice:

- Gershwin, Porgy and Bess "Bess, You is My Woman Now" (soprano and bass)
  Compact Disc No. 4, Track 9
- Handel, Messiah "For Unto us a Child is Born" (choir)
  Cassette Tape, Side B, Example 6
  Compact Disc No. 1, Track 5
- Mussorgsky, Boris Godunov "Coronation Scene" (basso profondo)
  Compact Disc No. 3, Track 4
- Schubert, The Erlking (baritone and piano)
  Cassette Tape, Side C, Example 19
  Compact Disc No. 2, Track 6

- Schumann, Widmung (soprano and piano)
  Compact disc No. 2, Track 7
- Sondheim, A Little Night Music "Send in the Clowns" (soprano)
  Compact Disc No. 4, Track 12

Chapter 6 - Music Before 1600

Middle Ages:

- Guillaume de Machaut (c. 1300-1377): Notre Dame Mass

Renaissance:

- Josquin des Prez (c 1440-1521): motets
- Palestrina: Pope Marcellus Mass, motets
- Italian Madrigals: Gesualdo, Monteverdi
- English Madrigals: Morley

Chapter 8 - Baroque Music

J.S. Bach:

- Cantata No. 4, "Christ lag in Todesbanden" (Christ lay in the bonds of death)
- Cantata No. 80, "Ein' feste Burg" (A Mighty Fortress)
- Cantata No. 140, "Wachet auf" (Sleepers Awake)
- St. Matthew Passion
- Christmas Oratorio
- Mass in b minor
- Magnificat in D
- Brandenburg Concertos 1-6
- 4 Orchestral Suites
- harpsichord concertos
- violin, cello, and flute sonatas
- Well-Tempered Clavier
- Goldberg Variations

Handel:

- Messiah oratorio
- Israel in Egypt oratorio
- Giulio Cesare opera
- Music for the Royal Fireworks
- Water Music Suites
- chamber music

Monteverdi:

- madrigals
- <u>Orfeo</u>

D. Scarlatti:

- sonatas for harpsichord

A. Scarlatti:

- sonatas for harpsichord

Schutz:

- Italian madrigals
- <u>The Seven Words from Christ on the Cross</u>

Vivaldi:

- <u>The Four Seasons</u> (four concertos)
- solo concertos
- <u>Gloria</u>

Chapter 10 - Music of the Classical Period

Mozart:

- <u>Symphonies</u>: No. 31 (Paris)
No. 35 (Haffner)
No. 36 (Linz)
No. 38 (Prague)
No. 39
No. 40 (g minor)
No. 41 (Jupiter)

- <u>Piano Concertos</u>: No. 15, K. 450
No. 17, K. 453
No. 18, K. 456
No. 21, K. 467
No. 23, K. 488

- <u>String Quartets</u>: "Six Haydn Quartets" K. 387, K. 421, K. 428, K. 458, K. 464, K. 465
<u>Serenade</u> "Eine kleine Nachtmusik" K. 525

- <u>Piano Music</u>: sonatas, variations, fantasias

- Mass: Requiem Mass

- Operas: Die Entfuehrung aus dem Serail (The Abduction from the Harem)
  La nozze di Figaro (The Marriage of Figaro)
  Don Giovanni
  Cosi fan tutte (Women are Like That)
  Die Zauberflöte (The Magic Flute)

Haydn:

- Symphonies: No. 92 (Oxford)
  No. 94 (Surprise)
  No. 100 (Military)
  No. 101 (Clock)
  No. 104 (Drum Roll)

- Chamber Music: Op. 54, 54, 55, 64, 71, 74, 76
  piano trios, string trios

- Oratorios: Die sieben letzten Worte (The Seven Last Words)
  Die Schöepfung (The Creation)
  Die Jahreszeiten (The Seasons)

Beethoven (early):

- Symphonies: No. 1 in C Major, Op. 26
  No. 2 in D Major, Op 36
  No. 3 (Eroica) in E-Flat Major, Op. 55
  No. 5 in C Minor, Op 67

- Piano Concertos: No. 3 in C Minor, Op. 37
  No. 5 (Emperor) in E-Flat Major, Op. 73

- String Quartets: Op. 18

Chapter 11 - Beethoven: Bridge to Romanticism

Beethoven:

- Symphonies: No. 6 (Pastorale) in F Major, Op. 68
  No. 7 in A Major, Op. 92
  No. 9 (Choral) in D Minor, Op. 125

- Overtures: Egmont Overture
  Leonore Overtures No. 1-3

- Violin Concerto: Violin Concerto, Op. 61

- String Quartet: Op. 59, No. 1-3

- Piano Sonatas: No. 8, Op. 13, "Pathétique"
No. 14, Op. 27, No. 2, "Moonlight"
No. 21, Op. 53, "Waldstein"
No. 23, Op. 57, "Appassionata"

- Violin Sonatas: No. 5, Op. 24, "Spring"
No. 9, Op. 47, "Kreutzer"

Chapter 13 - Early Romantic Music

Berlioz:

- Harold in Italy, Op. 16 (viola and orchestra)
- Symphonie fantastique, Op. 14
- Roman Carnival Overture
- Requiem

Chopin:

- Piano Concertos No. 1 and No. 2
- Piano Music

Duparc: Songs

Fauré: Songs

Greig: Songs

Liszt:

- Les Préludes (for orchestra)
- Faust Symphony
- Piano Concertos No. 1 and No. 2
- Piano Music

Mendelssohn:

- Symphony No. 3 (Scottish)
- Symphony No. 4 (Italian)
- Symphony No. 5 (Reformation)
- A Midsummer Night's Dream Overture
- Hebrides [Fingal's Cave] Overture
- Violin Concerto

- Ruy Blas Overture
- Songs and Piano Music

Schubert:

- Symphony No. 8 (Unfinished)
- Symphony No. 9 (Great)
- Incidental Music to Rosamunde
- "Death and the Maiden" String Quartet
- "The Trout" String Quartet
- "Ave Maria" (song)
- Die Forelle (song: The Trout)
- Die Schöne Müllerin (song cycle)
- "Winterreise" (song cycle)

Schumann:

- Symphony No. 1 (Spring)
- Piano Concerto in A Minor
- "Papillons" (piano)
- "Carnival" (piano)
- "Dichterliebe" (song cycle)

Chapter 14 - Romantic Opera

Bellini:

- I puritani
- La sonnambula
- Norma

Bizet:

- Carmen

Donizetti:

- La Fille du Regiment (The Daughter of the Regiment)

Gounod:

- Faust

Offenbach:

- Tales of Hoffman

Puccini:

- La Bohème
- Madame Butterfly
- Tosca
- Turandot

Rossini:

- The Barber of Seville
- William Tell

Wagner:

- Die Meistersinger von Nürnberg
- Die Walküre
- Parsifal

Weber:

- Der Freischütz

Chapter 15 - Late Romantic Music

Brahms:

- 4 Symphonies
- Piano Concerto No. 1 in D Minor
- Piano Concerto No. 2 in B-Flat Major
- Violin Concerto
- Academic Festival Overture
- Tragic Overture
- A German Requiem
- Alto Rhapsody (1869)
- chamber music
- piano music
- songs

Mahler:

- Symphony No. 1 (The Titan)
- Symphony No. 4
- "Lieder eines fahrenden Gesellen" (Songs of a Wayfarer)
- "Das Lied von der Erde" (The Song of the Earth)

Strauss, R.:

- Horn Concerto No. 1 in E-Flat
- Horn Concerto No. 2 in E-Flat
- Oboe Concerto
- Salome (opera)
- Der Rosenkavalier (The Cavalier of the Rose, opera)
- Die Frau ohne Schatten (The Woman without a Shadow, opera)
- Four Last Songs (with orchestra)
- songs with piano

Wagner: See recommendations in Chapter 14.

Program Music:

Beethoven:

- Symphony No. 6 (Pastoral) in F Major, Op. 68

Berlioz:

- Harold in Italy, Op. 16 (viola and orchestra)
- Symphonie fantastique, Op. 14

Liszt:

- Symphonic Poems: Hamlet and Les Préludes
- Dante Symphony
- Faust Symphony

Mendelssohn:

- Midsummer Night's Dream Overture
- Calm Sea and Prosperous Voyage Overture
- Hebrides [Fingal's Cave] Overture

Strauss, R.:

- Also Sprach Zarathustra (Thus Spoke Zarathustra)
- Death and Transfiguration
- Don Juan
- Don Quixote
- Ein Heldenleben (A Hero's Life)
- Till Eulenspiegel's Merry Pranks

Tchaikovsky:

- 1812 Overture
- Francesca da Rimini
- Romeo and Juliet

Chapter 16 - Nationalism

Russia:

Mussorgsky:
- A Night on Bald Mountain
- Pictures at an Exhibition
- Boris Godunov

Rimsky-Korsakov:
- Scheherazade
- Capriccio espagnol

Borodin:
- In the Steppes of Central Asia
- Prince Igor: "Polovtsian Dances"

Tchaikovsky:
- 1812 Overture
- Swan Lake, ballet music
- Piano Concerto No. 1
- Violin Concerto
- Symphonies 4-6

Rachmaninov:
- Piano Concerto No. 2

Hungary:

Bartók:
- Concerto for Orchestra
- Music for Strings, Percussion, and Celesta

Liszt:
- Hungarian Dances

Czechoslovakia:

Dvorák:
- Carnival Overture, Op. 92
- Concerto for Cello and Orchestra, Op. 104
- Quartet No. 12 in F Major, Op. 96 (American)

- Slavonic Dances
- Symphony No. 9 in E Minor, Op. 95 (New World)

Smetana:
- The Bartered Bride, opera and overture
- The Moldau, symphonic poem

Scandinavia:

Grieg:
- Concerto in A Minor for Piano and Orchestra, Op. 16
- Peer Gynt Suite, No. 1 and No. 2, Op. 46 and 55
- songs

Sibelius:
- Concerto in D Minor for Violin and Orchestra, Op. 47
- Finlandia, Op. 26
- Swan of Tuonela, Op. 22
- Symphony No. 2 in D Major, Op. 43
- Valse triste

United Kingdom:

Elgar:
- Enigma Variations, Op. 36
- Pomp and Circumstance Marches (5), Op. 39

Vaughan Williams:
- Fantasia on "Greensleeves"
- English Folk Song Suite
- "London" Symphony

Grainger:
- "Irish Tune from County Derry"
- Lincolnshire Posy (for wind band)

Italy:

Respighi:
- Fountains of Rome
- Pines of Rome
- The Birds

Spain:

Albéniz:
- Iberia
- Suite Española

Granados:
- Spanish Dances (12)

Falla:
- El amour brujo
- Nights in the Gardens of Spain
- Three Cornered Hat, ballet dances

Chapter 17 - Impressionism

Debussy:

- Clair de lune (for piano)
- Images pour Orchestre
- La Mer
- Nocturnes (for orchestra)
- String Quartet in G Minor
- Sonata No. 1 (for cello and piano)
- Sonata No. 3 (for violin and piano)
- Syrinx (for unaccompanied flute)

Ravel:

- Alborada del gracioso
- Bolero
- Concerto in G Major for Piano and Orchestra
- Daphnis et Chloé: Suite No. 2
- Pavane pour une infante défunte (for orchestra)
- String Quartet in F Major
- La Valse

Chapter 19 - Stravinsky: Into the Twentieth Century

Stravinsky:

- Circus Polka
- "Dumbarton Oaks" Concerto
- "Ebony" Concerto
- Firebird Suite
- Fireworks
- L'histoire du soldat (The Soldier's Tale)
- Octet (for winds)
- Petrushka (ballet)
- Pulcinella suite
- The Rake's Progress
- Le sacre du printemps (The Rite of Spring)
- Symphony of Psalms

Chapter 20 - Expressionism: Atonal Music

Berg:

- Concerto for Violin and Orchestra
- Lyric Suite (for string orchestra)
- Quartet, Op. 3
- Sonata for Piano, Op. 1
- Three Pieces for Orchestra, Op. 6
- Wozzeck

Schoenberg:

- Chamber Symphony, Op. 9
- Concerto for Violin and Orchestra, Op. 42
- Erwartung, Op. 17
- Five Pieces for Orchestra
- Gurre-Lieder
- Moses und Aron (opera)
- Pierrot lunaire, Op. 21
- String Quartets
- Serenade for Septet and Baritone, Op. 24
- Suite for Chamber Ensemble
- Survivor from Warsaw, Op. 46
- Variations for Orchestra, Op. 31
- Verklaerte Nacht, Op. 4

Webern:

- Five Movements for String Quartet, Op. 5
- Four Pieces for Violin and Piano, Op. 7
- Quartet for Clarinet, Tenor Saxophone, Piano, and Violin, Op. 22
- Symphony for Chamber Orchestra, Op. 21
- Variations for Piano Solo, Op. 27

Chapter 21 - Neoclassicism: Mainstream Music

See listings for each composer.

Chapter 22 - Experimental and Technological Music

Musique Concrete:

The Beatles: "Mr. Kite"
"Tomorrow Never Knows"
"Revolution No. 9"

Reich: Come Out

Stockhausen: Gesang der Jünglinge
(speech sounds and electronic sounds)

Electronic Music:

Carlos: By Request
Switched on Bach (CBS MS-7194)

Subotnik: Silver Apples of the Moon

Varese: Poèm éléctronique

Wuorinin: Time's Ecomium

Computer Mixed Media:

Boulez: Regions

Davidosky: Synchronisms No. 5

Dodge: In Celebration

Risset: Songs

Aleatoric Music:

Eloy: Equivalences

Stockhausen: Klavierstück XI

Chance Music:

Cage: Atlas Eclipticalis

Xenakis: Pithoprakta

Chapter 23 - Music in the United States

See works cited under each composer.

Chapter 26 - Music for Films

- The Adventures of Robin Hood (1938), music by Erich Korngold
- Accidental Tourist, music by John Williams
- Altered States, music by John Corigliano
- Anastasia, music by Alfred Newman
- Anatomy of a Murder, music by Duke Ellington

- The Bad and the Beautiful, music by David Raksin
- Batman, music by Danny Elfman
- Beaches, music by Georges Delerue
- Betrayed, music by Bill Conti
- Born on the Fourth of July, music by John Williams
- Breakfast at Tiffany's, music by Henry Mancini
- A Clockwork Orange, music by Wendy (Walter) Carlos
- Cocoon, music by James Horner
- Dr. Zhivago, music by Maurice Jarre
- Driving Miss Daisy, music by Hans Zimmer
- Elmer Gantry, music by Andre Previn
- The Empire Strikes Back, music by John Williams
- E.T. (The Extraterrestrial), music by John williams
- Eye of the Needle, music by Miklos Rozsa
- Fantasia, music by Stravinsky, Beethoven, and others
- Field of Dreams, music by James Horner
- 48 Hours, music by James Horner
- Friendly Persuasion, music by Dmitri Tiomkin
- The Godfather, music by Nino Rota
- Glory, music by James Horner
- Gone with the Wind, music by Max Steiner
- Gremlins, music by Jerry Goldsmith
- Harry and the Hendersons, music by Bruce Broughton
- In the Heat of the Night, music by Quincy Jones
- Jaws, music by John Williams
- Koyaanisqatsi, music by Phillip Glass
- Laura, music by David Raksin
- Lethal Weapon, music by Michael Kamen
- Louisiana Story, music by Virgil Thomson
- Moonwalker, music by Bruce Broughton
- Midnight Cowboy, music by John Barry
- Napoleon, music by Carmine Coppola
- The Natural, music by Randy Newman
- Octopussy, music by John Barry
- Of Mice and Men, music by Aaron Copland
- On the Waterfront, music by Leonard Bernstein
- Out of Africa, music by John Barry
- The Pink Panther, music by Henry Mancini
- Poltergeist, music by Jerry Goldsmith
- Presidio, music by Jerry Goldsmith
- Prizzi's Honor, music by Alex North
- Raiders of the Lost Ark
- Red Pony, music by Aaron Copland
- The Right Stuff, music by Bill Conti
- Rocky I, II, III, music by Bill Conti
- Sayonara, music by Franz Waxman
- Separate Tables, music by David Raskin
- Shaft, music by Quincy Jones

- Silverado, music by Bruce Broughton
- Sophie's Choice, music by Marvin Hamlisch
- Spellbound, music by Miklos Rozsa
- Starman, music by Jack Nitzsche
- Star Trek, music by Jerry Goldsmith
- Star Wars, music by John Williams
- Steel Magnolias, music by Georges Delerue
- Summerand Smoke, music by elmer Bernstein
- Superman (and sequels), music by John Williams
- Swann in Love, music by Hans Werner Henze
- Sweet Liberty, music by Bruce Broughton
- Time after Time, music by Niklos Rozsa
- The Tin Drum, music by Maurice Jarre
- Twins, music by Georges Delerue
- Victory at Sea, music by Richard Rogers
- Witness, music by Maurice Jarre
- The Woman in Red, music by Stevie Wonder
- Young Lions, music by Hugo Friedhofer
- Young Sherlock Holmes, music by Bruce Broughton

Chapter 27 - Contributions of World Cultures

Records or tapes of authentic world culture music are difficult to obtain. Some university and public libraries have recordings. some stores may stock these recordings. To find out what recordings are available, consult the Schwann Catalog found at most record stores.

The following two-record set is recommended as a listener's introduction to world music:

- The Nonesuch Explorer, H7-11 (stereo, 2-record set)

Recordings on The Nonesuch Explorer illustrate world music from the European continent as well as music from many distant lands including

- Bali (Indonesia)
- Japan (including Kabuki, shakuhachi, and koto music)
- India (folk music and Northern and Southern classical music)
- Columbia
- Brazil
- Peru
- Paraguay
- Mexico
- Trinidad
- Bahamas

Paul Horn:

"Inside the Taj Mahal" (KUK LP 1062)
"Inside the Great Pyramids" (KUK LP and CD 060/61)
"China" (KUK CD 080)

Appendix B

Summary of Composers

Chapter 6 - Music Before 1600

Middle Ages - See Composer Summary for Middle Ages.

Renaissance - See Composer Summary for Renaissance.

Chapter 8 - Baroque Music

Bach, Johann Sebastian (1685-1750)
Buxtehude, Dietrich (c. 1637-1707)
Couperin, Francois (1668-1733)
Handel, George Frideric (1685-1759)
Gabrieli, Giovanni (1557-1612)
Monteverdi, Claudio (1567-1643)
Rameau, Jean-Philippe (1683-1764)
Scarlatti, Alessandro (1660-1725)
Scarlatti, Domenico (1685-1757)
Schütz, Heinrich (1585-1672)
Teleman, Georg Philipp (1681-1767)
Vivaldi, Antonio (1678-1741)

Chapter 10 - Music of the Classical Period

Beethoven, Ludwig van (1770-1827)
Haydn, Franz Joseph (1723-1809)
Mozart, Leopold (1719-87)
Mozart, Wolfgang Amadeus (1756-91)
Salieri, Antonio (1750-1825)

Chapter 13 - Early Romantic Music

Berlioz, Hector (1803-69))
Chopin, Frédéric (1810-49)
Czerny, Karl (1791-1857)
Duparc, Henri (1848-1933)
Fauré, Gabriel (1845-1924)
Grieg, Edvard (1843-1907)
Liszt, Franz (1811-86)
Mendelssohn, Felix (1805-47)
Schubert, Franz (1797-1828)
Schumann, Clara (1819-96)
Schumann, Robert (1810-56)
Wolf, Hugo (1860-1903)

Chapter 14 - Romantic Opera

Bellini, Vincenzo (1801-35)
Bizet, Georges (183875)
Cherubini, Luigi (1760-1842)
Gounod, Charles (1818-93)
Meyerbeer, Giacomo (1791-1864)
Offenbach, Jacques (1819-80)
Puccini, Giacomo (1858-1924)
Rossini, Gioacchino (1792-1868)
Spontini, Gasparo (1774-1851)
Strauss, Johann, Jr. (1825-99)
Sullivan, Arthur (1842-1900)
Thomas, Ambroise (1811-96)
Verdi, Giuseppe (1813-1901)
Wagner, Richard (1818-83)
Weber, Carl Maria von (1786-1826)

Chapter 15 - Late Romantic Music

Brahms, Johannes (1833-97)
Mahler, Gustav (1860-1911)
Strauss, Richard (1864-1949)
Tchaikovsky, Peter Ilyich (1840-93)
Wagner, Richard (1813-83)

Chapter 16 - Nationalism

Albéniz, Issac (1860-1909)
Balakirev, Mily (1837-1910)
Bartók, Béla (1881-1945)
Borodin, Alexander (1833-87)
Cui, César (1835-1918)
Dvorák, Antonin (1841-1904)
Elgar, Edward (1857-1934)
Falla, Manuel de (1876-1947)
Grainger, Percy (1882-1961
Granados, Enrique (1867-1916)
Grieg, Edvard (1867-1916)
Kabalevsky, Dmitri (1904-87)
Khachaturian, Aram (1903-78)
Kodály, Zoltán (1882-1967)
Liszt, Franz (1811-86)
Mussorgsky, Modest (1839-81)
Prokofiev, Sergi (1891-1953)
Puccini, Giacomo (1858-1924)
Rachmaninov, Sergei (1873-1943)
Respighi, Ottorino (1879-1936)

Rimsky-Korsakov, Nikolai (1844-1908)
Scriabin, Alexander (1872-1915)
Shostakovitch, Dmitri (1906-75)
Sibelius, Jan (1865-1957)
Smetana, Bedrich (1824-84)
Tchaikovsky, Peter Ilyich (1840-93)
Vaughan Williams, Ralph (1872-1958)
Verdi, Giuseppi (1813-1901)

Chapter 17 - Impressionism

Debussy, Claude (1862-1918)
Ravel, Maurice (1875-1937)

Chapter 20 - Expressionism: Atonal Music

Berg, Alban (1885-1935)
Schoenberg, Arnold (1874-1951)
Webern, Anton (1887-1945)

Chapter 21 - Neoclassicism: Mainstream Music

Chavez, Carlos (1899-1978)
Elgar, Edward (1858-1935)
Grainger, Percy (1882-1961)
Hindemith, Paul (1895-1963)
Holst, Gustav (1874-1935)
Honegger, Arthur (1892-1955)
Kabalevsky, Dmitri (1904-87)
Khachaturian, Aram (1903-78)
Kodáy, Zoltán (1882-1967)
Milhaud, Darius (1892-1974)
Orff, Carl (1895-1959)
Poulenc, Francis (1899-1963)
Prokofiev, Sergei (1891-1953)
Rachmaninov, Sergei (1872-1943)
Respighi, Ottorino (1879-1936)
Satie, Erik (1866-1925)
Shostakovich, Dmitri (1906-1975)
Stravinsky, Igor ((1882-1971)
Vaughan Williams, Ralph (1872-1958)
Villa-Lobos, Heitor (1887-1959)
Weill, Kurt (1900-50)
Walton, William (1902-83)

Chapter 22 - Experimental and Technological Music

Babbitt, Milton (b. 1916)
Boulez, Pierre (b. 1925)
Brown, Earle (b. 1926)
Cage, John (b. 1912)
Carlos, Wendy (Walter, b. 1939)
Davidovsky, Mario (b. 1934)
Dodge, Charles (b. 1942)
Feldman, Morton (1926-89)
Foss, Lukas (b. 1922)
Glass, Philip (b. 1937)
Lesemann, Frederick (b. 1936)
Luening, Otto (b. 1900)
Penderecki, Krysztof (b. 1933)
Reich, Steve (b. 1936)
Stockhausen, Karlheinz (b. 1928)
Subotnick, Morton (b. 1933)
Ussachevsky, Vladimir (b. 1911)
Varèse, Edgard (1883-1965)
Wolff, Christian (b. 1934)
Wuorinen, Charles (b. 1938)
Xenakis, Iannis (b. 1922)
Young, LaMonte (b. 1935)

Chapter 23 - Music in the United States

Barber, Samuel (1910-81)
Bartók, Béla (1881-1945)
Bernstein, Leonard (1918-1990)
Copland, Aaron (b. 1900)
Gershwin, George (1898-1937)
Gottschalk, Louis (1829-69)
Hanson, Howard (1896-1981)
Hindemith, Paul (1895-1963)
Ives, Charles (1874-1954)
Joplin, Scott (1868-1917)
Mahler, Gustav (1860-1911)
Menotti, Gian Carlo (b. 1911)
Milhaud, Darius (1894-1974)
Piston, Walter (1894-1976)
Schoenberg, Arnold (1874-1951)
Schuman, William (b. 1910)
Sessions, Roger (1896-1985)
Stravinsky, Igor (1882-1971)
Zwilich, Ellen Taaffe (b. 1939)

Chapter 24 - American Popular Music

Arlen, Harold (b. 1905)
Baez, Joan (b. 1943)
Berlin, Irving (1888-1989)
Blake, Eubie (1883-1984)
Denver, John (b. 1943)
Dylan, Bob (b. 1941)
Emmett, Dan (1815-1904)
Foster, Stephen (1826-64)
Gershwin, George (1898-1937)
Handy, W.C. (1873-1958)
Kern, Jerome (1885-1945)
Lennon, John (1940-82)
McCartney, Paul (b. 1942)
Porter, Cole (1891-1964)
Rodgers, Richard (1902-79)
Seeger, Pete (b. 1919)
Simon, Paul (b. 1942)
Stevens, Cat (b. 1948)

Chapter 25 - American Musical Theater

Adler, Richard (b. 1921)
Berlin, Irving (1888-1989)
Bernstein, Leonard (1918-1990)
Blake, Eubie (1883-1983)
Bland, James (1854-1911)
Bock, Jerry (b. 1928)
Cohan, George M. (1878-1942)
Ebb, Fred (b. 1932)
Foster, Stephen (1826-64)
Friml, Rudolph (1879-1972)
Gershwin, George (1898-1937)
Hamlisch, Marvin (b. 1944)
Harnick, Sheldon (b. 1924)
Herbert, Victor (1859-1924)
Herman, Jerry (b. 1933)
Jones, Tom (b. 1928)
Kern, Jerome (1885-1945)
Lane, Burton (b. 1912)
Leigh, Mitch (b. 1928)
Lerner, Alan Jay (1918-86)
Loesser, Frank (1910-69)
Porter, Cole (1891-1964)
Rodgers, Richard (1902-79)
Ross, Jerry (1926-55)

Schmidt, Harvey (b. 1929)
Schoenberg, Claud-Michel (b. 1947)
Sondheim, Stephen (b. 1928)
Styne, Jule (b. 1905)
Webber, Andrew Lloyd (b. 1948)
Weill, Kurt (1900-50)
Willson, Meredith (1902-84)
Youmans, Vincent (1898-1946)